A-Z SCOTLAND

REFERENCE

Motorway	**M8**
Under Construction	
Proposed	
Motorway Junctions with Numbers	
Unlimited Interchange **4**	Limited Interchange **5**
Motorway Service Area (with fuel station)	**HAMILTON** Ⓢ
with access from one carriageway only	Ⓢ
Major Road Service Areas (with fuel station)	**DREGHORN**
with 24 hour facilities	Ⓢ
Primary Route (with junction number)	**A50** 32
Primary Route Destination	**OBAN**
Dual Carriageways (A & B Roads)	
Class A Road	**A814**
Class B Road	**B9080**
Major Roads Under Construction	
Major Roads Proposed	
Fuel Station	
Gradient 1:5(20%) & Steeper (Ascent in direction of arrow)	
Toll	*Toll*
Mileage between Markers	8
Railway and Station	
Level Crossing and Tunnel	
River or Canal	
County or Unitary Authority Boundary	
National Boundary	
Built-up Area	
Village or Hamlet	
Wooded Area	
Spot Height in Feet	· 813
Relief Above 400' (122m)	
National Grid Reference (Kilometres)	800
Area Covered by Town Plan	**SEE PAGE 102**

TOURIST INFORMATION

Airport		
Airfield		
Heliport		
Battle Site and Date		
Castle (open to public)		
Castle with Garden (open to public)		
Cathedral, Abbey, Church, Friary, Priory		✝
Country Park		
Ferry (vehicular)		
(foot only)		
Garden (open to public)		✳
Golf Course	9 Hole	18 Hole
Historic Building (open to public)		
Historic Building with Garden (open to public)		
Horse Racecourse		
Lighthouse		
Motor Racing Circuit		
Museum, Art Gallery		
National Park		
National Trust for Scotland	(open)	NTS
	(restricted opening)	NTS
Nature Reserve or Bird Sanctuary		
Nature Trail or Forest Walk		
Place of Interest	Monument ·	
Picnic Site		
Railway, Steam or Narrow Gauge		
Theme Park		
Tourist Information Centre		
Viewpoint	(360 degrees)	
	(180 degrees)	
Visitor Information Centre		V
Wildlife Park		
Windmill		
Zoo or Safari Park		

SCALE

0 1 2 3 4 5	10 Miles
0 1 2 3 4 5	10
	16 Kilometres

Map Pages 4-90
1:221,760
3.5 Miles to 1 Inch

EDITION 4   2024

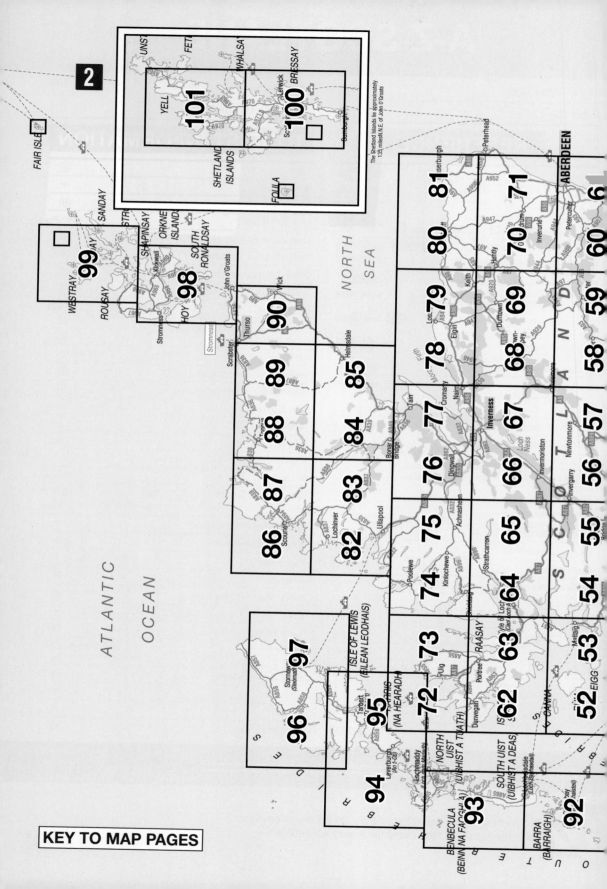

KEY TO MAP PAGES

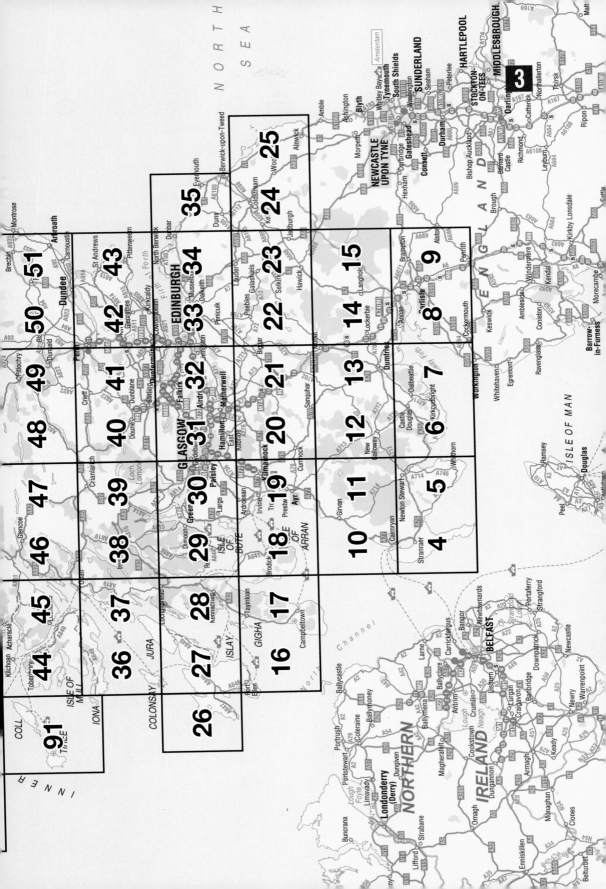

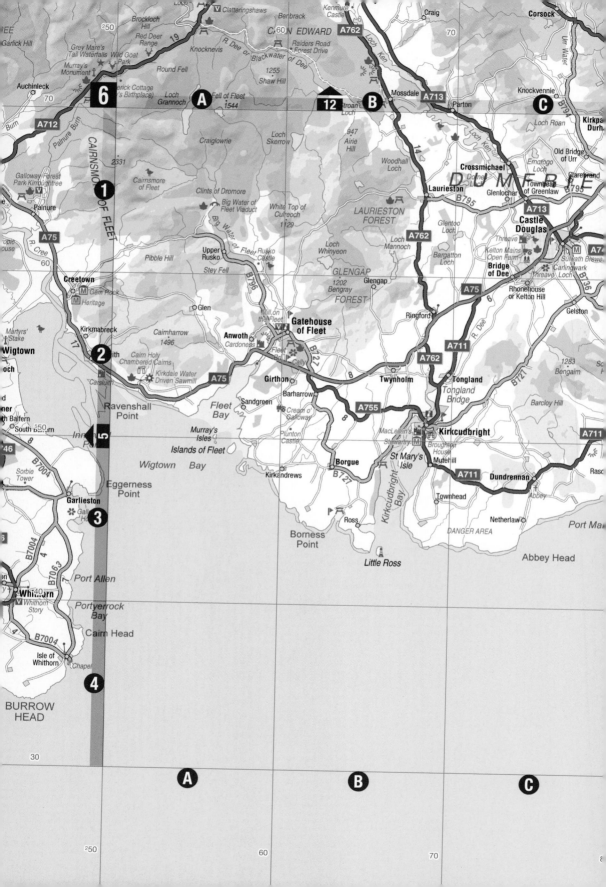

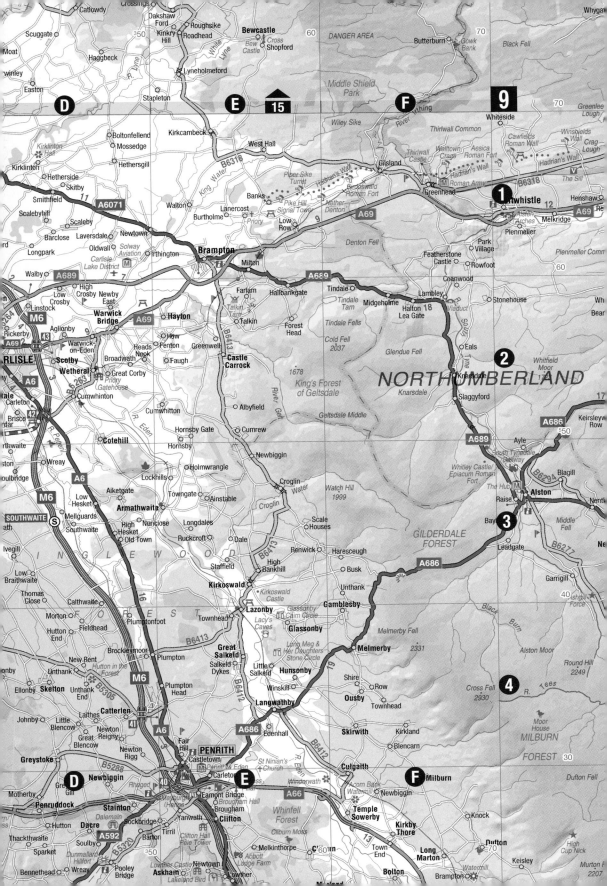

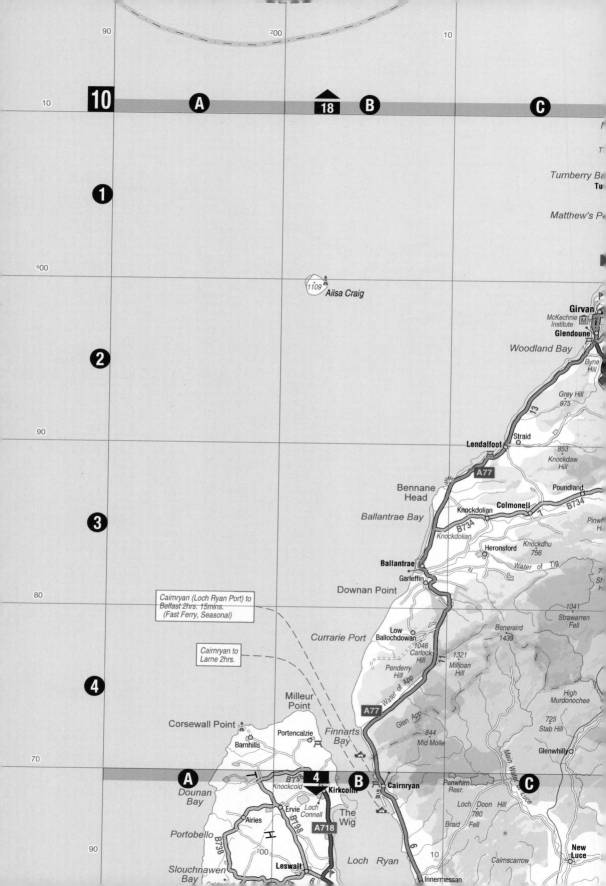

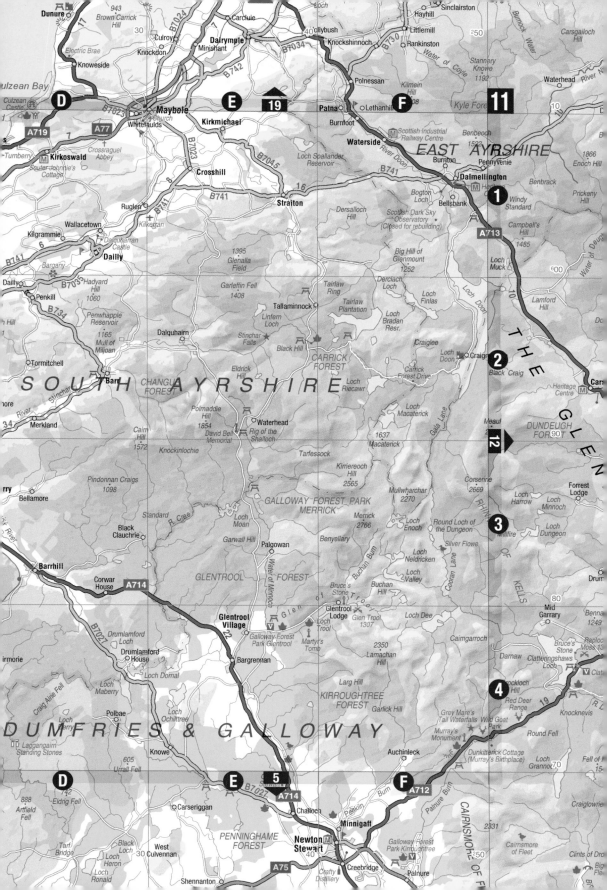

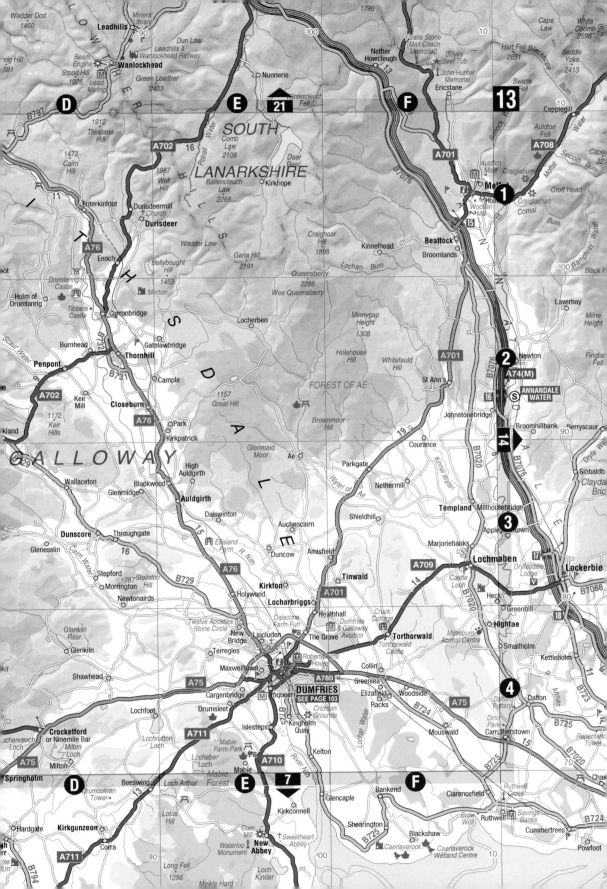

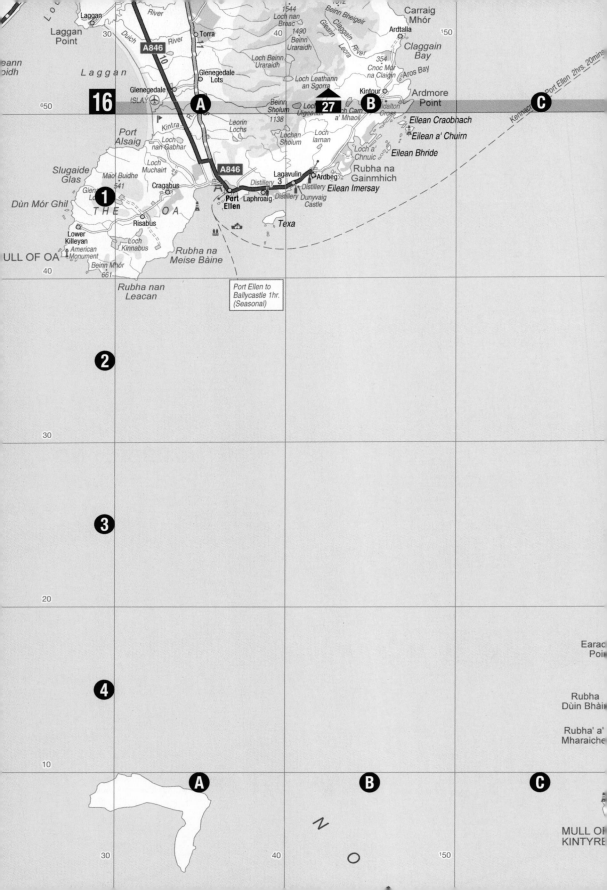

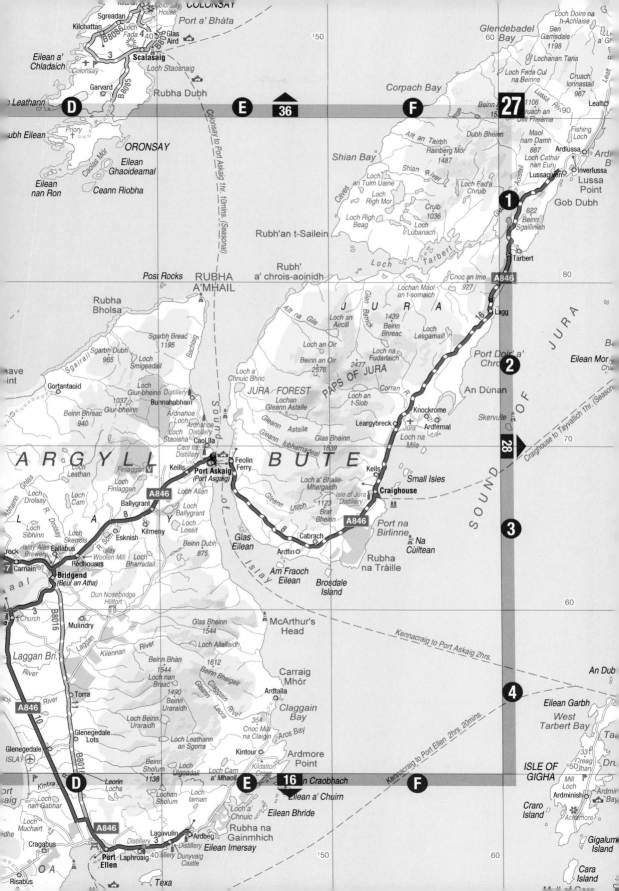

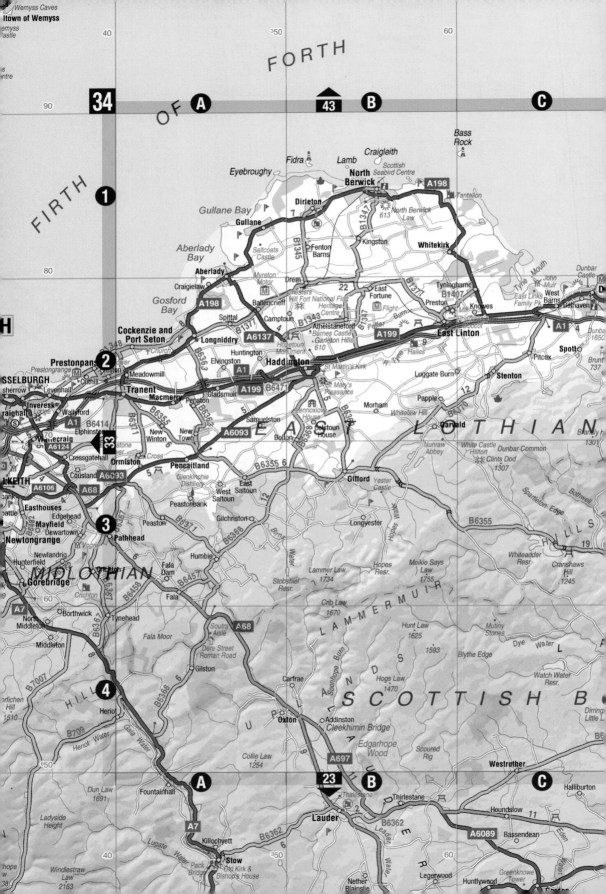

D **E** **F**

1

2

3

4

N O R T H   S E A

Barns Ness
East Barns
Skateraw
...erton
Power Station
Thorntonloch
...nnerwick
8
Cocklaw Hill 1046
Dunglass Collegiate Church
Reed Point
Cove
Siccar Point
Cockburnspath
Oldhamstocks
Fast Castle Head
Fast Castle
Telegraph Hill
Lumsdaine
Cross Law 744
ST ABB'S HEAD
St Abbs
Lifeboat Station
803 Meikle Black Law
Blackburn Rig
A1107
Coldingham Moor
11
Coldingham
Priory
Coldingham Bay
Lifeboat Station
283
...rt Law
A1
Grantshouse
Houndwood
Eye Water
B6438
Eyemouth
Gunsgreen House
M
M
Gunsgreenhill
Abbey St Bathans
A6112
859 Herseley Hill
Reston
18
Ayton
A1107
Burnmouth
Ross
60
...s
Water
Ellemford
Edin's Hall Broch
B6438
Auchencrow
B6437
B6355
B6355
B6355
A1
Whitchester
M
Millburn Bridge
B6355
Lintlaw
B635
Chirnside
12
Lamberton
Marshall Meadows
...macus
M
B6365
Preston
Cumledge Mill
Chirnsidebridge
Arch
Edrom
Tithe Barn
Clappers
Halidon Hill 1333
Manderston
M
Whiteadder Water
Foulden
SCOTLAND
A6105
4
Cell Block
BERWICK-UPON-TWEE
...RDERS
Jim Clark Room
M
Duns
A6105
Allanton
B6437
Hutton
Paxton
ENGLAND
A6105
B6461
Castle
M
M
Tweedmouth
Lifeboat Station
Spittal
Gavinton
Nisbet Hill
B6460
Whitsome
B6461
Fishwick
Tweed
Union Bridge
Loanend
East Ord
A1167
650
Polwarth
A6112
Chain Bridge
Honey
A698
Po...
Doodle Do
Redshin Cove
D
A6105
Fogo
Fogorig
B6460
E
24
Horndean
B6461
Horncliffe
F
Murton
Scremerston
B6354
Greenlaw
Charterhall
Ladykirk
Norham
Thornton
West Allerdean
B6525
Cheswick
M E R S E
80
B6461
Swinton
A6112
12
Simprim
Upsettlington
90
Grindon
Felkington
400
Ancroft
Gos...
A697
10
Leitholm
B6437
Twizel Bridge
Duddo Stone Circle
Berrington Law
Haggerston

IONA

Réidh Eilean

Eilean Annraidh

Maclean's Cross
Iona Heritage Centre
Baile Mór
Sound of Iona
10mins

tac an 'pineidh

lean nah-Aon Chaorach

Greave

Soa land

ROSS OF MULL

Rubha nan Cearc

Kintra

Creich

Aridhglas

Fionnphort

Poit na h-I

Fidden

Erraid

Knockvologan

Eilean nam Muc

Eilean a' Chalmain

Torran

Sgeir Dhoirbh

Staffa
Fingal's Cave

Little Colonsay

Erisgeir

Garbh Phort

Eorabus

Loch na Làthaich

Knockan

Beinn a' Ghlinne Mhoir

369 Ross of Mull Historical Centre

Bunessan

Loch Assopol

Ardalanish

Uisken

Ardchiavaig

Ardalanish Bay

Beinn a' Chaol-Airigh 411

Rubh' Ardalanish

Rubha nam Bràithrean

Inch Kenneth

Island

Chapel

Gribun

Derryc

B8035 17

BEN MORE 3171

Glen

Coirc Bheinn 1837

Corra-bheinn 2311

Rubha na h Uamha

MacCulloch's Fossil Tree

Tiroran

Tavool House

Port na Croise

B8036

ARDMEANACH

Creach Bheinn 1613

Beinn Bhreine 1704

Loch Scridain

Kilfinichen Bay

Pennyghael

Beinn na Croise 1649

Coladoir R

Loch Fuaran

Bun an Leoib

Ardchrishnish

A849 12

Torrans

BROLASS

Beinn Chreagach 1235

Beach River

Cruachan Min 1232

Aoineadh River

Carsaig

Carsaig Bay

Carsaig Arches

Malcolm's Point

FIRTH

Oban to Colonsay 2hrs 20mins

Port na Cuilce

Balnahard

Kiloran Bay

Caman Eoin 469

Port Ceann a' Gharraidh

Uragaig

Loch an Sgoltaire

Kiloran

B8086 Colonsay House

COLONSAY

Sgreadan

Port a' Bhàta

Kilchattan

B8086 Loch Fada 4

Glas Aird

Eilean a' Chladaich

Colonsay 3

Scalasaig

Loch Staosnaig

Garvard

B8085

Eilean Leathann

Rubha Dubh

Corpach Bay

Colonsay to Port Askaig 1hr 10mins (See

Dubh Eilean

ORONSAY

Caolas Mór

Eilean Ghaoideamal

Ceann Riobha

Eilean nan Ron

an Tairbh

Rainberg Mór 1487

Dubh

Shian Bay

Loch an Tuim Uaine

Shian River

Loch Right Mor

Caves

Loch Fac Chruibh

Loch Right Beag

Cruib 1036

A849 5

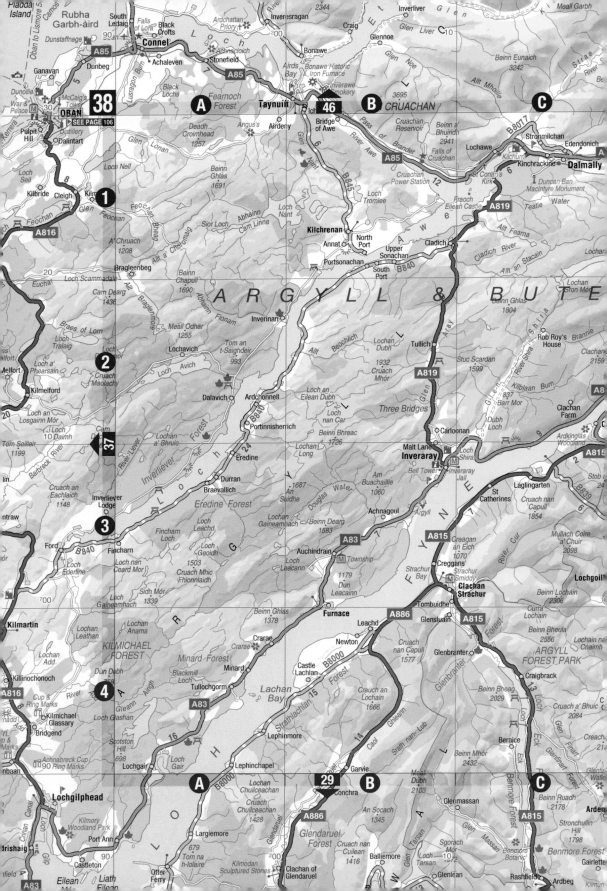

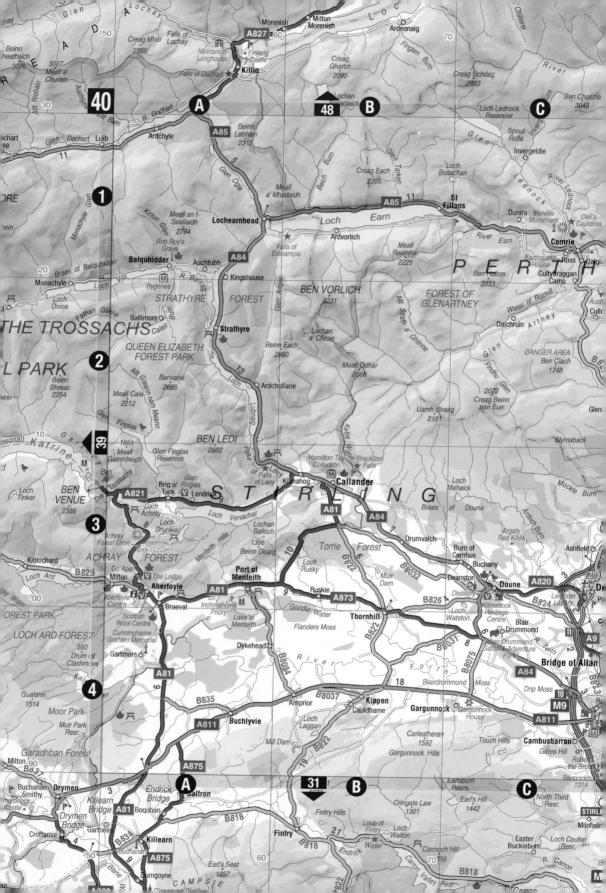

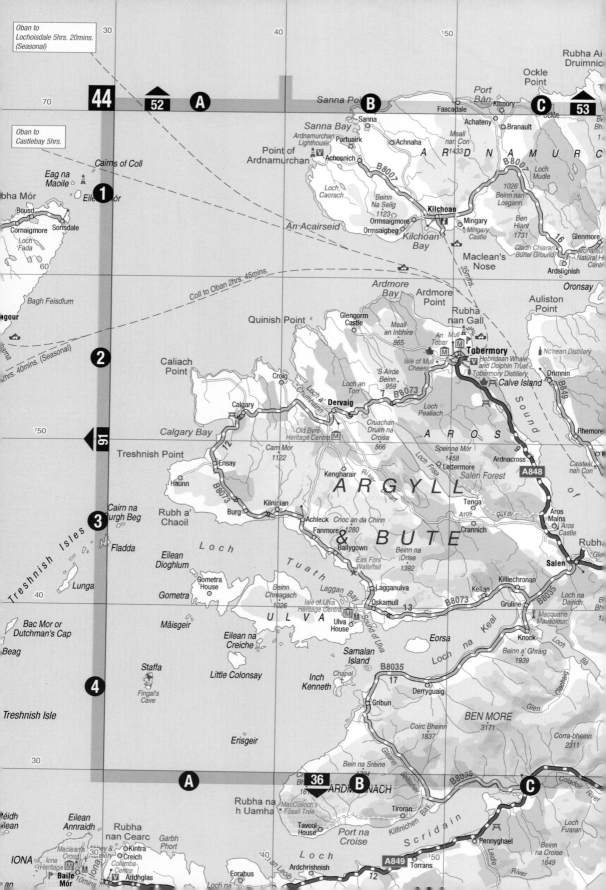

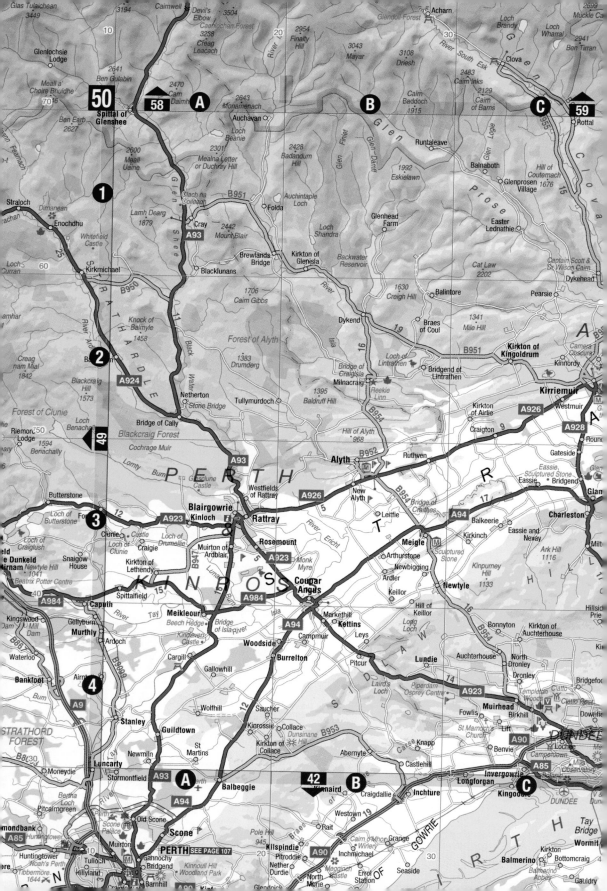

THE HEBRIDES

HEBR

❶

CANNA

Carn a'
Ghaill
693   Castle

Ceann Creag-
airighe

Garrisdale
Point   426   A' Chill   An
Coroghon   Canna Harbour

Rùm to Canna 55mins.   Ru
Shamhr

Kilmory

Kilmory Glen

Mullac
99

Sanday   Sound of Canna   Guirdil
Bay

Sgorr Mhór
1273   Kinloch

80 00   Orval
1874   Long
Loch   Lo
Gain

Schooner
Point   Sgorr Reidh   Glen Harris   Loch
Fiachanis

❷   Oigh-sgeir   RÙM
NATIONAL
NATURE RESERVE   Ainshval
2552

Ruinsival   Sgurr na
Gillean

90   Loch
Papadil

Rubha nam
Meirleach

SEA

❸   Eilean nan Ea

80   MUC

OF   Oban to
Lochboisdale 5hrs. 20mins.
(Seasonal)

❹   INNER

70   Ⓐ   **91**   Ⓑ   Ⓒ

Oban to
Castlebay 5hrs.   P
Ardri

Cairns of Coll

Eag na
Maoile
10   20   Rubha Mór   Eilean Mór   30

Bousd

Rubh'a' Rhinnin

Aberdeen to:
Kirkwall (Hatston) 6hrs.
Lerwick (Holmsgarth)
12hrs. 30mins.

NORTH

SEA

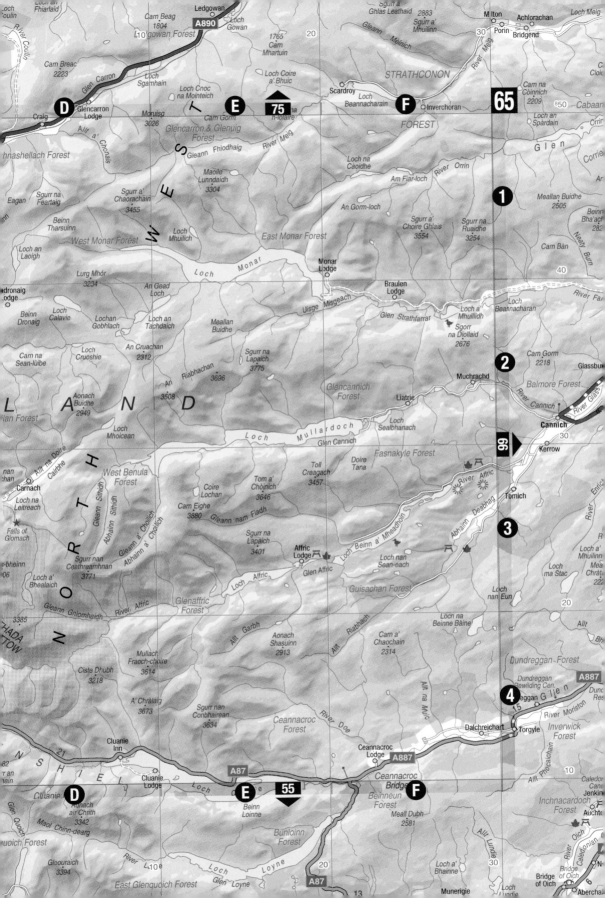

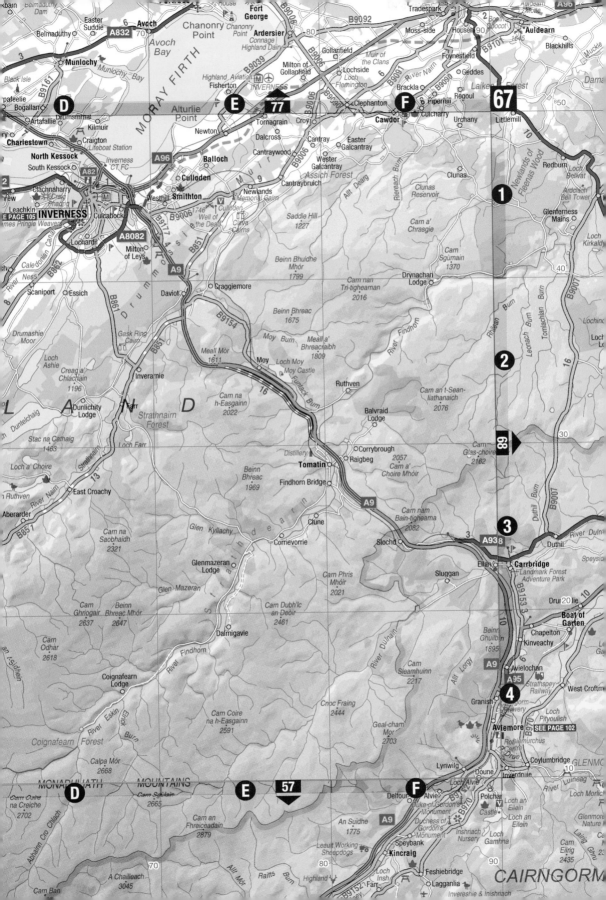

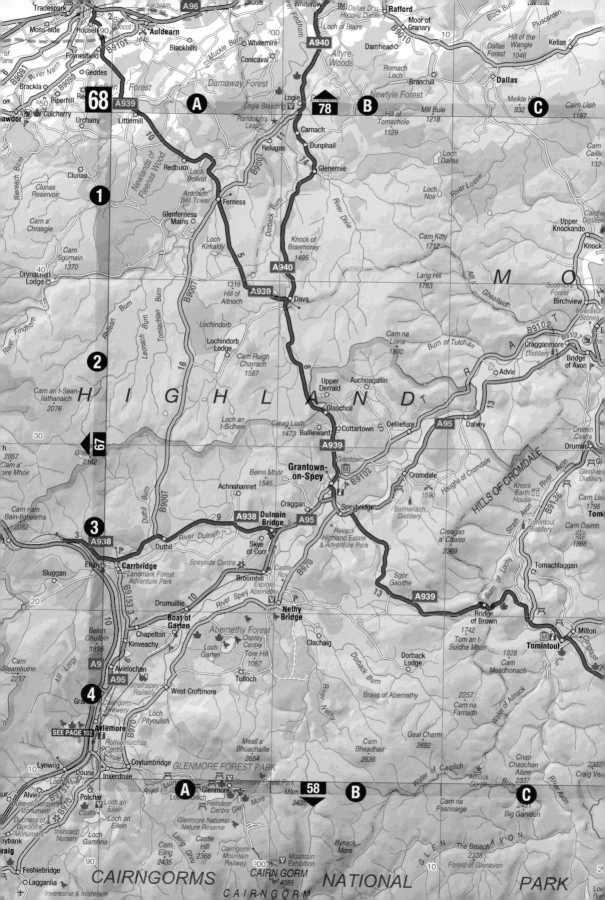

Eilean an Taighe

S

E

150   60   70

Rubha
Reidh

Camas
Mór

An Cu
972

1

Seana Chamas

Melvaig
Aultgrishan

Peterburn

Port Erradale   80rth
Erradale

Big Sand

Caolas Beag

Longa
Island

Loch

n Maol

Eilean
Troddaigh

Rubha na
h-Aiseig

Kilmaluag
Bay

The Aird

Shulista
m

Balmacqueen

2

**Port
Henderson**   9

B

Opinan   Loch nan

South
Erradale   70

River Erra

Redpoint

Kilmaluag

Connista

cdonald
ment

Flodigarry

Sgeir Eirin

Eilean Flodigarry

Staffin
Bay

Staffin Island

Sgeir Ghlas

74 ►

tair)
Loch
neosdal

1781·
Meall na
Suiramach

Quiraing
★   Digg
Glashvin

Cam Ban

Brogaig
Stenscholl

Garafad

Clachan

Staffin
(Stafainn)

3   na Trian

Rubha
na Fearn

Bioda
Buidhe
1523

Loch
Cleap

Staffin
Dinosaur

Kilt Rock
Mealt Falls

Ellishadder
Dun Grianan

M   Kilt Rock

Fearnmore   Fearnbeg   60

Maligar

Loch
Mealt

Valtos

Rubha
Chuaig

Arinacrinachd

Marishader

Garros

Rubha nam
Brathairean

Cuaig

Kenmore
L
Ch

Conon

Beinn Edra
2006

Shilasdair
Natural Dye Co   Culnacnoc

Grealin

A855

Loch
a' Bhràige

Port an
Fhearainn

Abhainn Chuaig

t-Strathain

Loch
Gaineamhach

Balnaknock

Lealt River

Lealt   Lealt
Falls

RONA

Callakille

4

Lonbain

Cròic 2
161

inlich

Craig
Bhàin
1995

Leac
Tressirnish

Eilean
Garbh

An 50 h-loch

sdal
ge

Beinn
a' Sgà

Loch
Liuravay

**THE
STORR**

Old Man
of Storr
2358

S
O
U
N
D

O
F

R
A
A
S
A
Y

Eilean
Garbh

Garbh Eilean

I
N
N
E
R

S
O
U
N
D

mesdal   River   Romesdal

Eyre

Somaichean Coir'
Fhinn Standing Stones

River   Haultin

Beinn
a' Chearcaill

1812

Bearreraig
Bay

Holm
Island

Eilean Tigh

Caol Rona

Eilean
Fladday

Loch
a' Squirr

Loch
nan Eun

Loch
Applecross

Applecr
Fores

Kensaleyre

Rhenetra

Loch
Leathan

Manish
Point

Torran

Arnish

Arnish

River Applecross

Heritage
Centre   **M**

clach
Ard'
D

Crepkill

Borve

Borve Standing
Stones

Loch
Fada

Brochel   Brochel
Castle

keabost
Carbost

A87

A855

Uigshader

Drumuie

Achachork

150   Dun
Torvaig   rashader

Glam
Burn

70
Applecross
Bay

Applecross
Milton

Glengrasco

B885

Sr

Shulishadermor
(Sùlaisiadar Mòr)

Portree
(Port Righ)

B8021

B8021
9

90

Loch

N

T
R
O
T
T
E
R
N
I
S
H

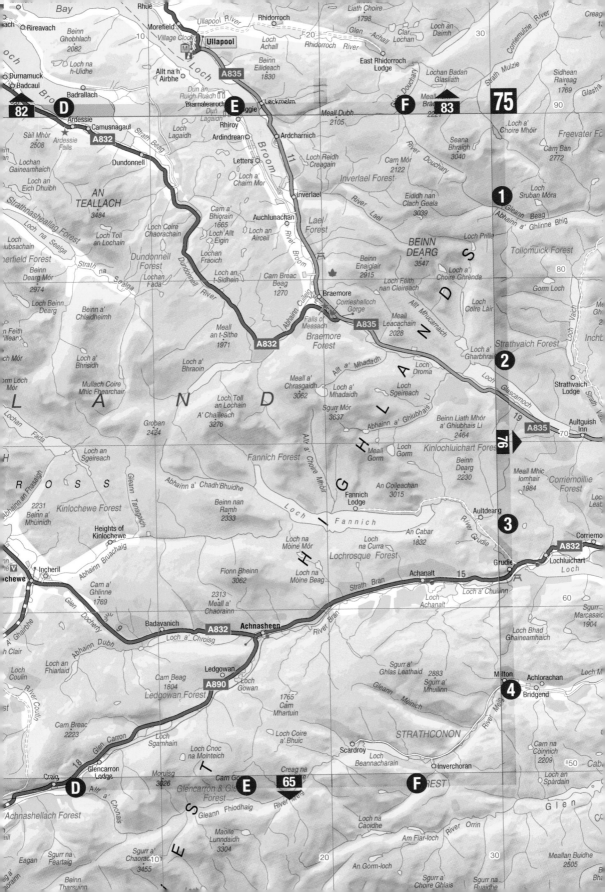

A
85
B
C

TARBAT NESS

Wilkhaven

Bindal

1

Portmahomack

Tarbat Discovery Centre

Seafield

Inver

Rockfield

Lower
Arboll

Toulvaddie

Tarrel

Low
Pitkerrie

Geanies

Hilton of
Cadboll Chapel

**Hilton of
Cadboll**

Balintore

2

Tullich

Shandwick

Clach a
Charridh

Port an Righ

77

3

N O R T H

Well

Hopeman

B9040

Covesea

Ca

Duffus

St Pet
Kir

Burghead

Cummingstown

Roseisle

B9012

Duf

K

Burghead Bay

Roseisle
Forest

College of
Roseisle

Quarrywood

Elg

Findhorn

Heritage
Centre

Findhorn
Foundation

B9011

Findhorn
Bay

Kinloss

B9089

17

Newton

12

Coltfield

Alves

Quarrel Wood
Woodland Park

Glen M
Distille

Miltonduff

Culbin Forest

Cloddymoss

Kintessack

Kinloss

Kinloss
Abbey

Moray

A96

Muir of
Miltonduff

Cran Loch

Broom
of Moy

Suegno's
Stone

B9011

Nelson Tower

Lochaber

Monaughty Forest

Heldon Hill
Pluscarden
Abbey

Foresterseat

Loch Loy

Rodney
Stone

Dyke

Brodie

FORRES

Califer

Barnhill

M O

Druim

Kingsteps

Balnageith

Falconer

Dallas Dhu
Historic Distillery

Rafford

Moor of
Granary

Black Burn

Pluscarden

Kellas

NAIRN

Tradespark

Whiterow

Whitemire

Damhead

B9010

Dallas
Forest

Hill of the
Wangie
1046

Moss-side

House

Boath
Doocot

Auldearn

Brodie

Loch of Blairs

Dallas

A96

7

HIGHLAND

Muckle Burn

Conicaval

Romach
Loch

Branchill

Newtyle Forest

Meikle Hill
932

Cairn Uish
1197

Foynesfield

Geddes

Blackhills

Druim

Darnaway Forest

Mill Buie
1218

Brackla

Piperhill

Regoul

Laiken
Forest

Logie

Drumine
Forest

Hill of
Tomechole
1129

Loch
Dallas

Carn na
Cailliche
1324

Culcharry

A939

Littlemill

Logie Steading

Randolph's
Leap

A940

A

68

B

C

Urquhary

Newlands of
Fleenas Wood

B9007

Refouls

Carnach

Dunphail

Loch
Noir

River Lossie

Cardhu
Distille

Redburn

Loch
Belivat

Glenernie

Upper
Knockandu

Clunas
Reservoir

Clunas

Ardclach
Bell Tower

Ferness

River Divie

Glenferness
Mains

Cam a'
Chracle

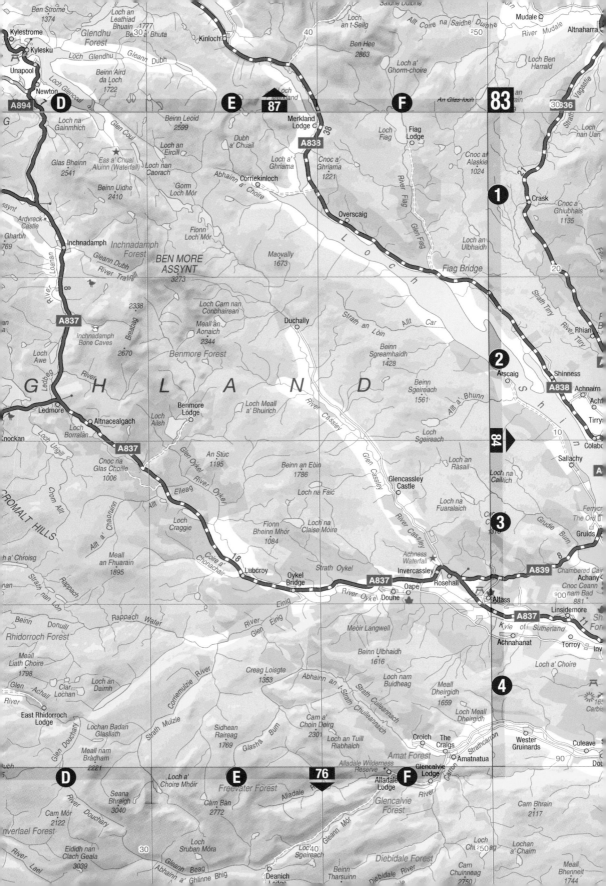

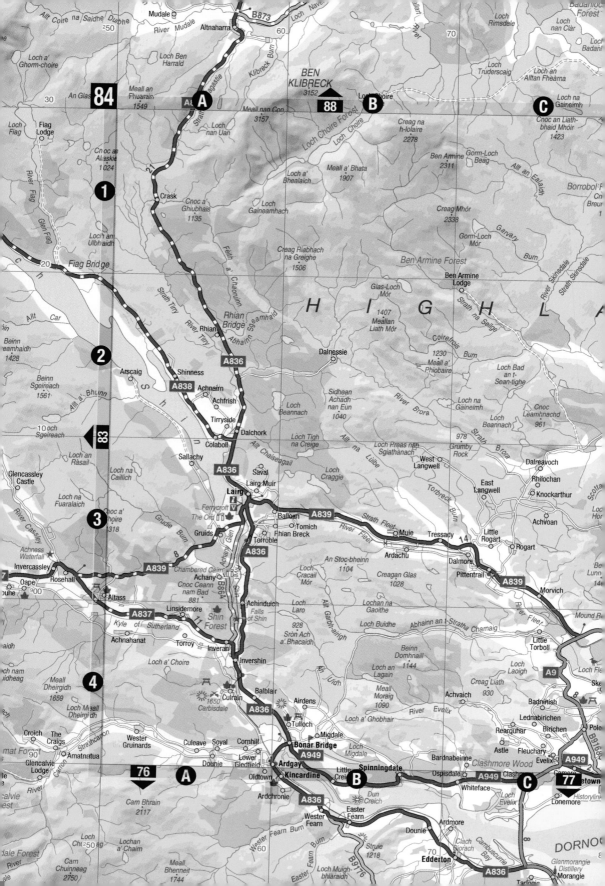

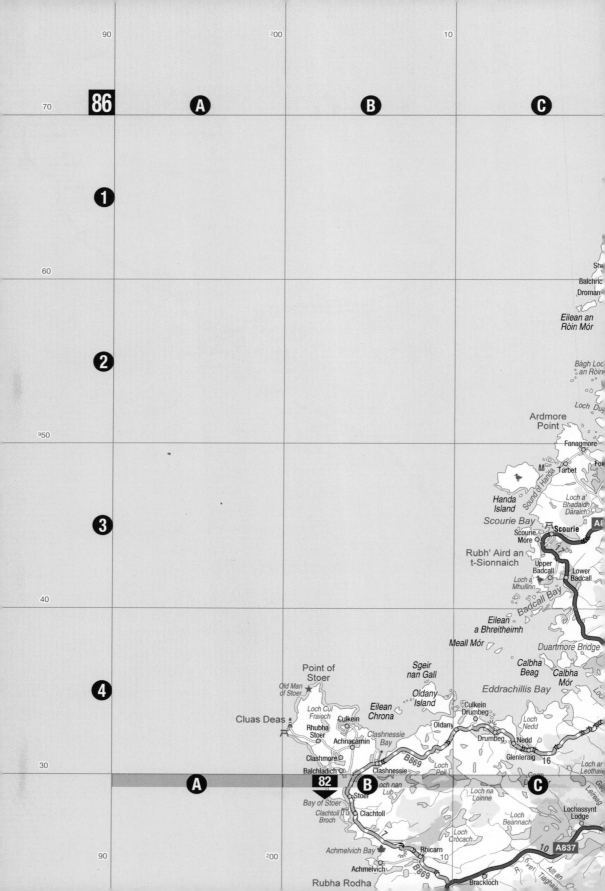

90   200   10

70   **86**   **A**   **B**   **C**

1

60

2

950

3

40

4

30

90   200

A   **82**   **B**   **C**

Sh
Balchric
Droman

Eilean an
Ròin Mór

Bàgh Loc
an Ròin

Loch Du

Ardmore
Point

Fanagmore

Tarbet   Fo

Handa
Island

Loch a'
Bhadaidh
Dàraich

Scourie Bay   Scourie   A&

Scourie
More

Rubh' Aird an
t-Sionnaich

Upper
Badcall

Lower
Badcall

Loch a'
Mhuilinn

Badcall Bay

Eilean
a Bhreitheimh

Meall Mór

Duartmore Bridge

Calbha
Beag

Calbha
Mór

Sgeir
nan Gall

Eddrachillis Bay

Point of
Stoer

Old Man
of Stoer

Oldany
Island

Culkein
Drumbeg

Loch Cùl
Fraioch

Eilean
Chrona

Loch
Nedd

Culkein

Cluas Deas

Rhubha
Stoer

Achnacarnin

Clashnessie
Bay

Oldany

Drumbeg

Nedd

Glenleraig

16

Loch ar
Leothai

Clashmore

Balchladich

B869

Clashnessie

Loch
Poll

82

Stoer

Loch nan
Lub

Loch na
Loinne

C

Lochassynt
Lodge

Bay of Stoer

Clachtoll
Broch

Clachtoll

Loch
Croçach

Loch
Beànnach

A837

Achmelvich Bay

Rhicarn

10

Achmelvich

B869

Rubha Rodha

Brackloch

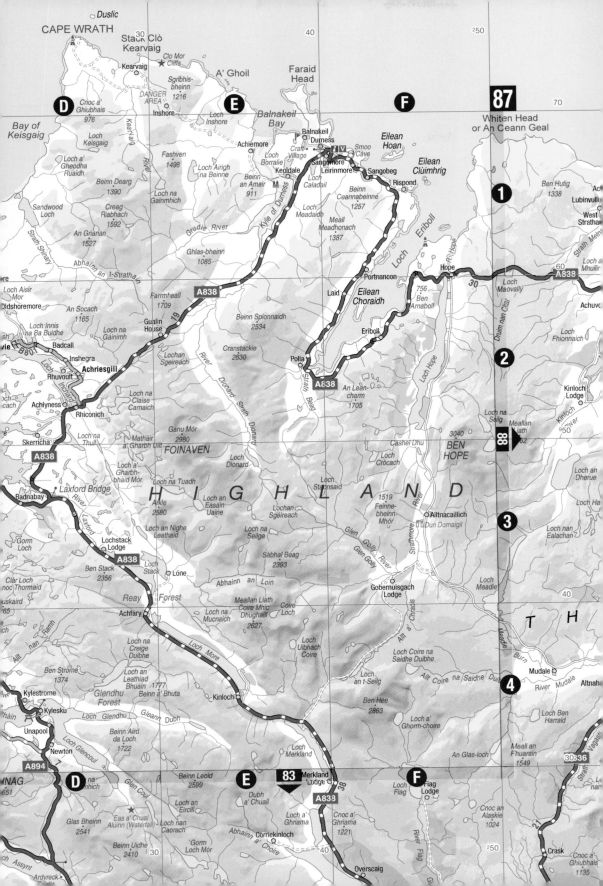

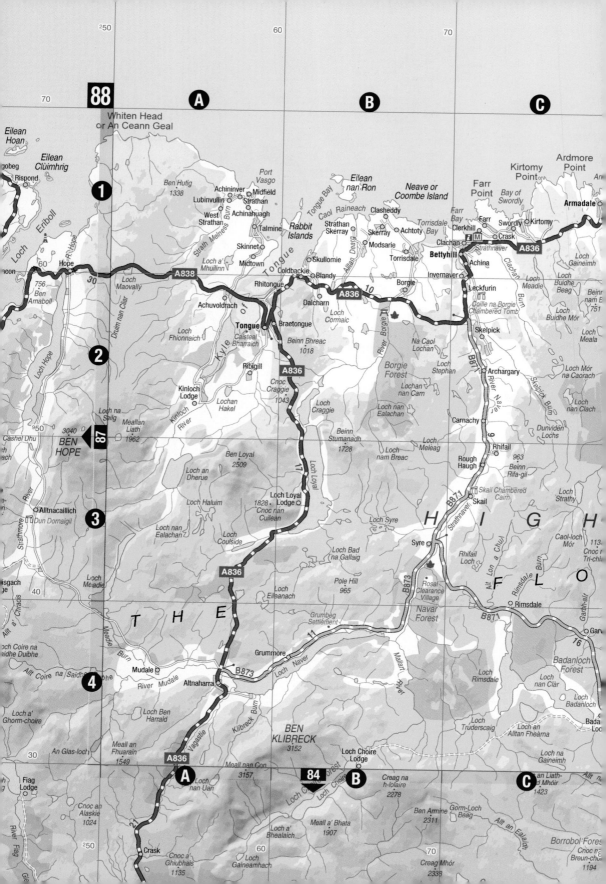

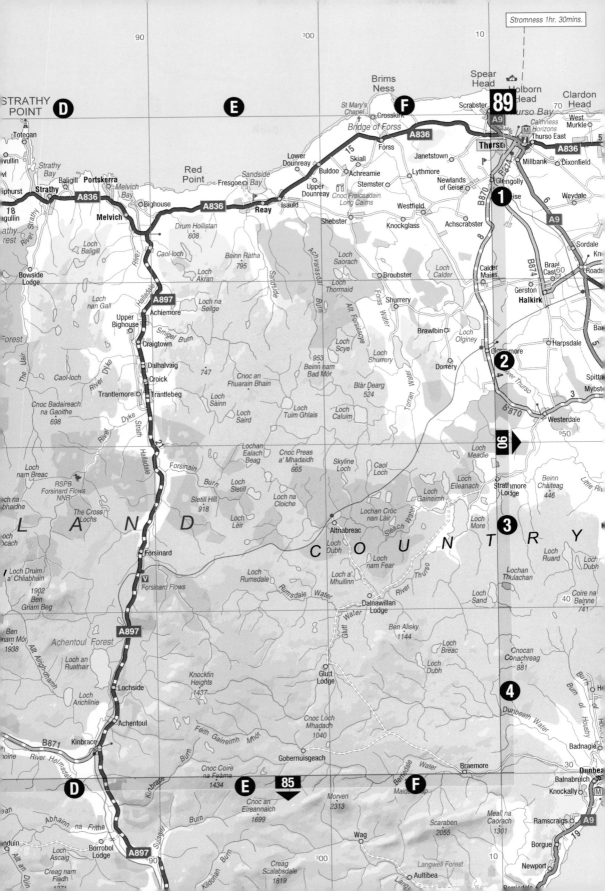

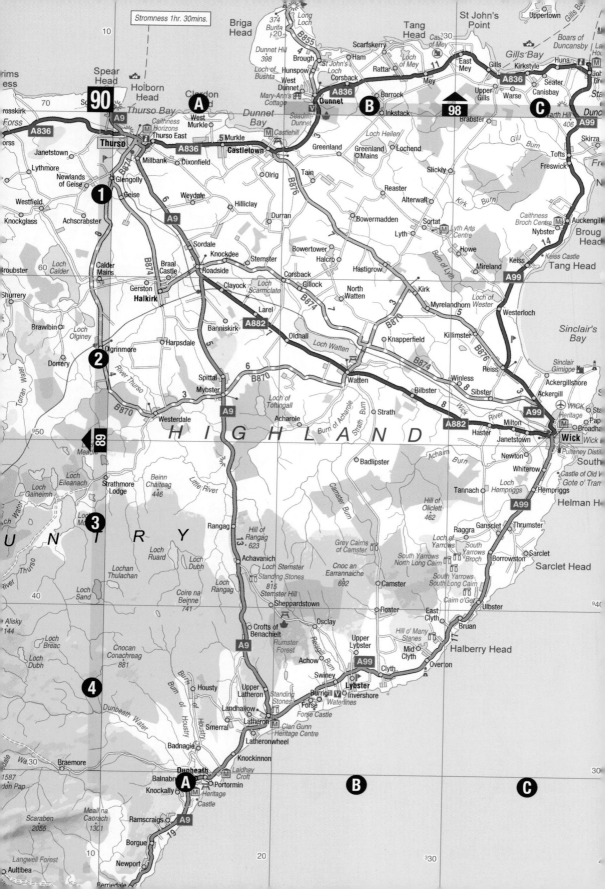

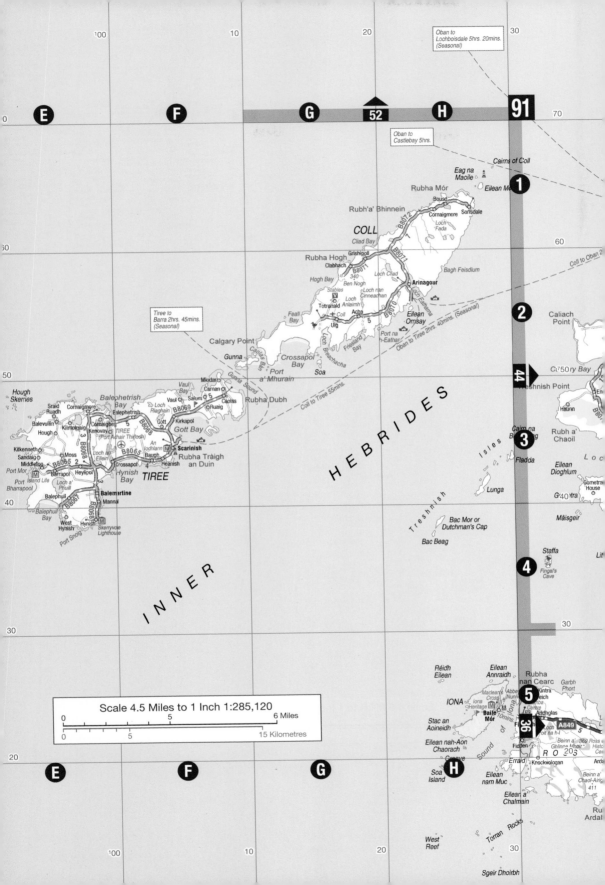

A **B** **C** **D**

Loch Bornish
Cill Loch a' Chlachain Loch Aineort
Donnain
Kildonan Calbhaigh Rubha
Bholuim
Taobh a Deas
Loch Aineort 80 Loch Aineort
Gearraidh M Mingearraidh
Bhailteas Aimeabhal
Frobost 822

Alsgernis Alsgerbheinn
Leathabhal
412 593 Loch Loch
Snigiscleit Stulabhal
Loch 1228 Stulaigh
Stulabhal
A865 Triuirebheinn
Dalabrog 1168

Ceann a Tuath
Loch Baghasdail Rubha
Cille Pheadair Creige Móire

20 Lochboisdale Lochoisdal
(Loch Baghasdail) Loch Baghasdail Mallaig 3hrs
Baghasdal 30mins, (S
Ceann a Deas Loch Calbhaigh Oban 5hrs.
Loch Baghasdail Chearsanais Rubha Meall 20mins. (S
Orasaigh an Tobha
An t-eth Loch
Meadhanach Easabhal Marulaigh
Gearraidh Gleann Dail Loch Rubha na
ma Monadh bho Dheas Móraibh 356 h-Ordaig
Smeircleit Ciilie Roineabhal 661
Bhrighde Ludag 10
Taobh a
Chaolais Calbhaigh
Lineigh Oitin a' Mhuillinn Thairteamul
Lineigh Caolas Eiriosgaigh Haunn 610
Am Baile ERISKAY
Acairseid 403 Coilleag (Eiriosgaigh)

WESTERN ISLES
(NA H-EILEANAN AN IAR)

Fiaraidh
Gob An Caolas Fiarach
Sgurabhal SOUND OF BARRA
Eolaigearraidh (An Caolas Barrach)

An Caolas Fuideach Fuday
Orasaigh (Fuideigh)
291 Na Stacar
Dubha

Ceann An Oitir Mhór Hellisay
Aird Ghrèin (Theilisigh)
Beinn BARRA Aird 311 Gighay
Eireabhal Mhór Caolas Theilisigh (Gioghaigh)
Cuidhir Claid Grein 680 Mhidhinis 242
Aird Fuideigh
Buaile nam Mhidhinis 352
Bodach Flodaigh
Bagh Bruairnis a Tuath
Gob A888 Shlarabhagh Bruairnis
Bhuirgh 309
BARRA Buaile nam
(Barraigh) Bodach Bruernish
Rubha Borgh A888 Sgallairidh Earsairidh Point
na Doirlinn Tangasdal Sheabhal Curachan
Beinn 1260 Breibhig Rubha
Tangabhal Kisimul Mór
1090 Castlebay
Caolas Bhatarsaigh (Bágh a' Chaistéil)
Biorueslum Caolas 624 Uidh
Theiseabhal Mór Bagh
Lingeigh Bhatarsaigh Uineasan
VATERSAY 279
(Bhatarsaigh) Bhatarsaigh Maol
Beinn Dòmhnaich
Ruilibhreac
Flodaigh Caolas Shandraigh
Càrn Ghaltair
678 Sandray
Lingeigh Greanamul (Sanndraigh)

Caolas Phabaigh

Pabbay An Tobha
(Pabaigh)
Theisgeir 561 Roisinis
a-muigh
Caolas Mhiùghlaigh

Cnoc
Mhic a' Phi
Mingulay 735
(Miùghlaigh) Bàgh
Mhiùghlaigh
Sheola
718 Bheàrnaraigh
Caolas
Berneray
(Beàrnaraigh)

Castlebay to:
Oban 5hrs.
Tiree 2hrs. 45mins.
(Seasonal)

Scale 4.5 Miles to 1 Inch 1:285,120

0 5 6 Miles
0 5 15 Kilometres

A **B** **C** **D**

Scale 4.5 Miles to 1 Inch 1:285,120

0   5   6 Miles

0   5   15 Kilometres

60   70   80   90

20   A   B   C   D

1

10

2

⁹00

3

90

4

80

5

70   A   93   B   C   D

WESTERN ISLES
(NA H-EILEANAN AN IAR)

Aird
Bhreinis

Camas a'
Greinaim

Eilean
Mhealas

Bràigh

Cearsta

Sron Romul
1012
SCARP

Hui

Rubha
Huisini

Hors

Glora
Tharan

Gàisgeir

Rub
Sgeir

TOE HEAD
(Gob an Tobha)

Rubh
a' C

Copaigh

Ceapabhal
1199

Siolaigh
Bheag

Siolaigh

Caolas Shiolaigh

Rubh' an
Teampaill

MacGill
Cen

An Tao
Tuath

Beinn a'
Charnain

Rubha Bhreinis

PABBAY
(Pabaigh) 643

Cuidhnis

Ensay
(Easaigh)
161

Caolas Spuir

Caolas Phabaigh

Boreray
(Boraraigh)

BERNERAY
(Beàrnaraigh)

Brusta

Ruisigearraidh

Baile

Borgh

Rhalteam

SOUND OF HIA

(Caolas Na Hearadh)

147 Ki
(Ceile

Rubha
Bhoisnis

Caolas Bheàrmaraigh

Sgeir a' Chàil

Opas

Haskeir Island
(Eilean Hasgeir)

Haskeir Eagach

Aird a'
Mhòrain

Rubha
Bheilis

Lingeigh

Orasaigh

Baile
MhicPhail

Port nan
Long

Siolait Mhic Neacail

Sursaigh

Taghaigh

Bhacas

Tobha-Beag

Amhlasaraigh

Bàgh a'
Chaise

Gro

Sgeallrabhal
332

Benn Mhor
824

Torogaigh

Loch
Mhic Phail

Rubha
Ghriminis

Valley
(Bhalaigh)

Scolpaig

A865

Griminis

Tràigh
Bhalaigh

Ceathramh
Meadhanach

Greinetobht

Trumaisgearraidh

Crògearraidh Mòr
588

A865

Lochportain

Rub
Dù

Rubha
Mhànais

Baile
Mhartainn

Taigh a'
Ghearraidh

Hogha
Gearraidh

Loch
Hosta

Cleitreabhal
a' Deas
435

Hosta

Malacleit

Solas

73

Loch nan
Geireann

Loch
Fada

Blathaisbhal

A865

Sruth Mòr

Loch
Sgeatar

Lochmaddy
(Loch na Madadh)

Taigh
Chearsabhagh

Loch nàm Madadh

Rubha an
Fhigheadair

Causamul

Aird an
Runair

Bàlranald

ghaill

NORTH UIST
(Uibhist a Tuath)

Maireabhal
755

Loch
Scadavay

Loch
Euphort

Rubha nam
Pleac

Rubh' Arnal

Paibeil

Baile Mòr

Ceann a'
Bhaigh

Deasker

Cladach a
Chàolais

Uineabhal
458

Loch
Huna

Loch nan Eun

Li a Tuath

Li a Deas
920

Rubha Port
Scolpaig

SOUND OF MONACH

(Caolas Mhonach)

Kirkibost Island
(Eilean Chircebost)

Cladach
Chircebost

Bhorogaigh

Cladach
Iolaraigh

A865

Barpa Langass
Chambered Cairn

Langais

Sornach Coir'
Fhinn Stone Circle

A867

Loch
Scadabhagh

Loch
Thundair

Loch
Carabhal

Loch
Obasaraigh

Huskeran

Ceann
Iar

Siolaigh 60

Stòcaidh

Heisker or Monach
Islands

Ceann
Ear

Teanna
Mhachair

Clachan
a' Luib

80

Hebridean Smokehouse

Samhla

A865

Baleshare
(Baile Sear)

Cairinis

Saighdinis

Loch
Euphort

Drium 90
Saighdinis

Eigneig Mhòr

An t-Aigeach

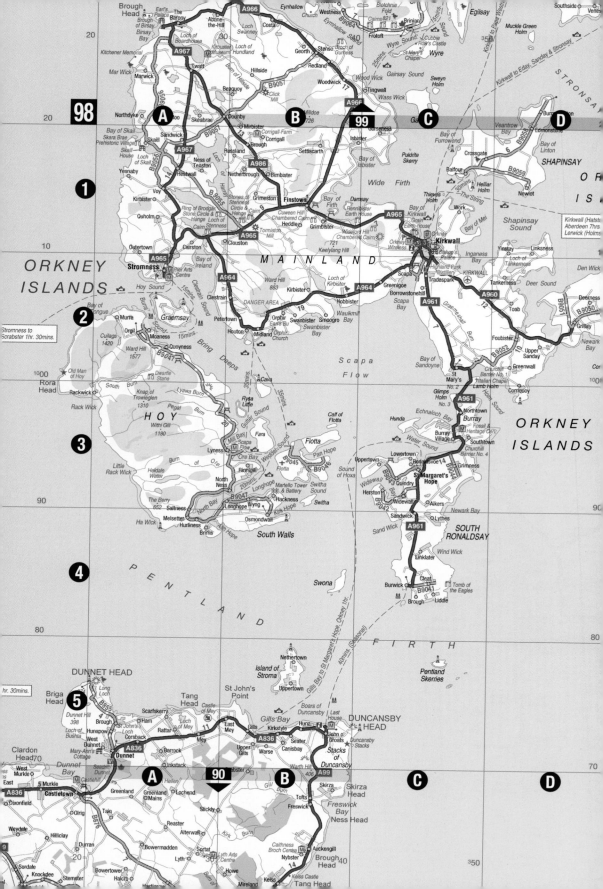

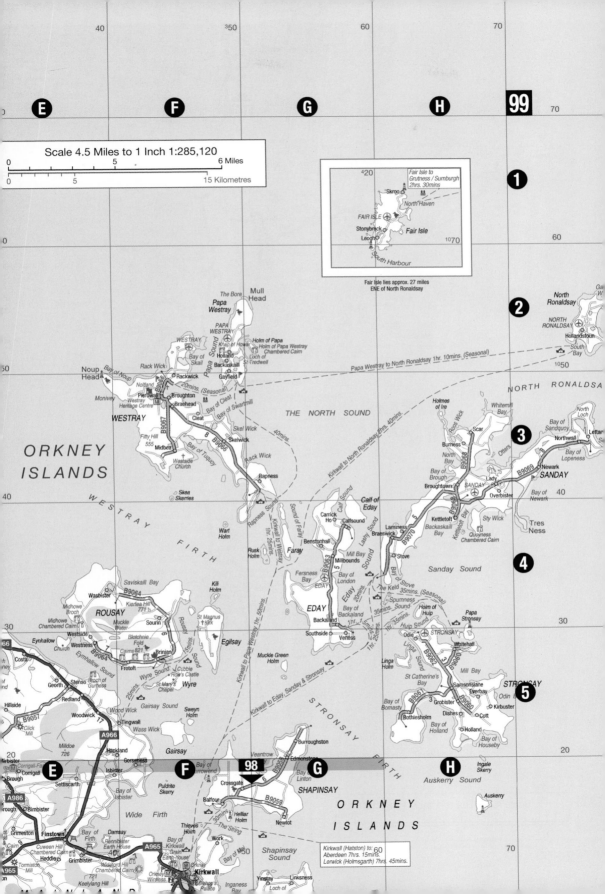

CITY & TOWN CENTRE PLANS

Reference to Town Plans

Motorway	**M8**	Abbey, Cathedral, Priory etc.	✝
Motorway Under Construction		Bus Station	➡
Motorway Junctions with Numbers	**4** **5**	Car Park (Selection of)	P
Unlimited Interchange **4** Limited Interchange **5**		Church	✝
Primary Route	**A82**	City Wall	ᒍᒐᒐᒐᒐ
Dual Carriageways		Ferry (vehicular) ⛴ (foot only) 🚶	
Class A Road	**A910**	Golf Course	
Class B Road	**B754**	Heliport	Ⓗ
Major Roads Under Construction		Hospital	Ⓗ
Major Roads Proposed		Lighthouse	🗼
Minor Roads		Market	
Fuel Station	⛽	National Trust Property (open) NT (restricted opening) NT	
Restricted Access		(National Trust for Scotland) NTS NTS	
Pedestrianized Road & Main Footway		Park & Ride	P+R
One Way Streets	➡	Place of Interest	■
Toll	Toll	Police Station	▲
Railway and Station	🚉	Post Office	★
Subway	⊖	Shopping Area (Main street and precinct)	
Level Crossing and Tunnel		Shopmobility	
Tram Stop and One Way Tram Stop		Toilet	▽
Built-up Area		Tourist Information Centre	🄻
		Viewpoint	☀ ☀
		Visitor Information Centre	Ⅴ

ABERDEEN

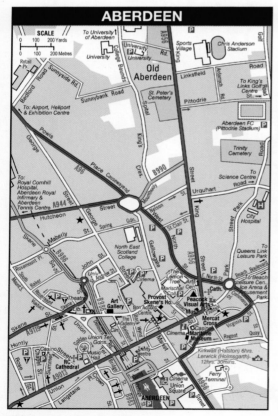

AVIEMORE

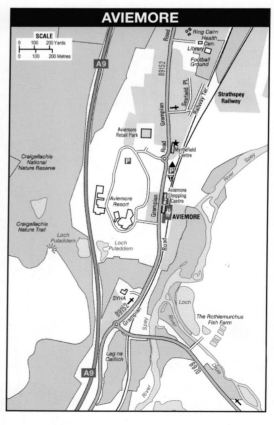

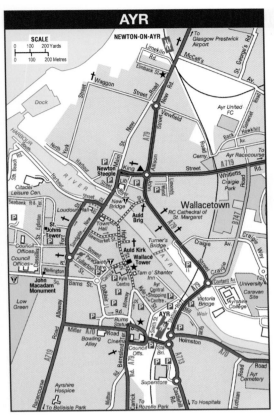

AYR

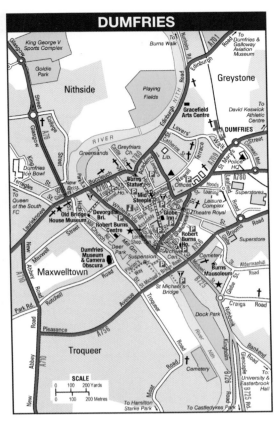

DUMFRIES

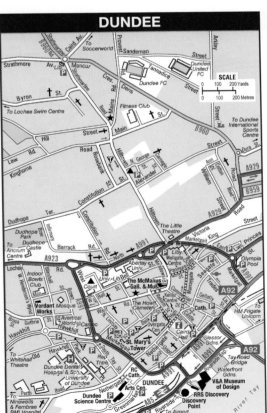

DUNDEE

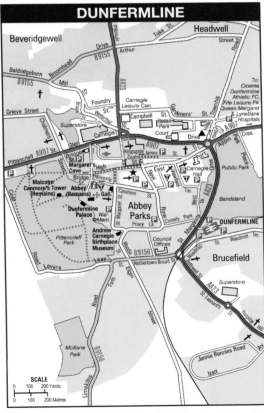

DUNFERMLINE

EDINBURGH

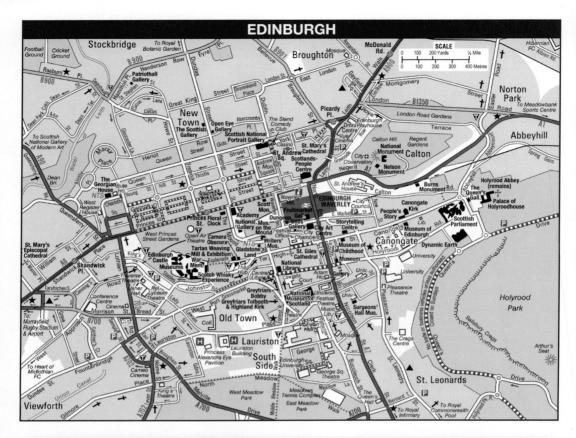

GLASGOW

FALKIRK

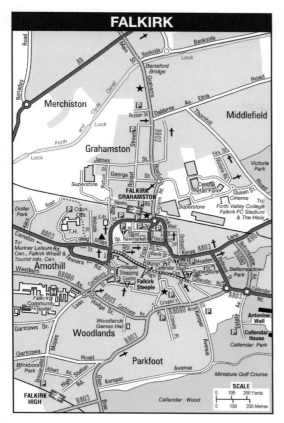

FORT WILLIAM

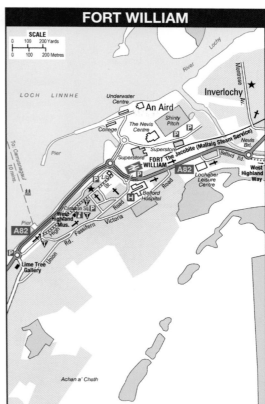

HAMILTON

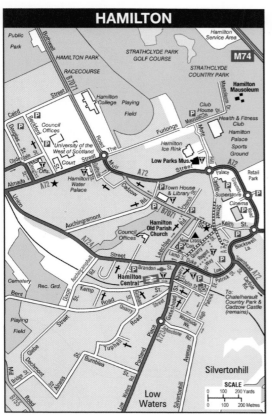

INVERNESS

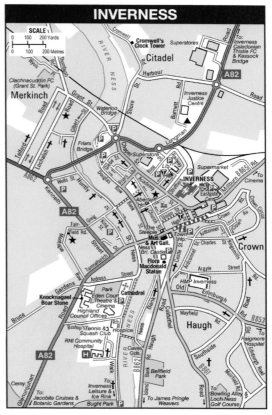

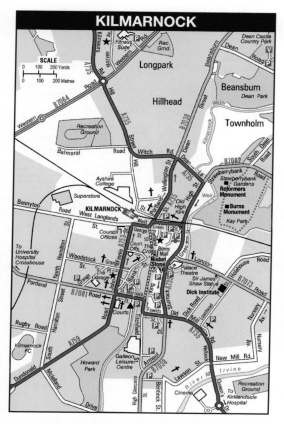

KILMARNOCK

SCALE
0 100 200 Yards
0 100 200 Metres

Dean Castle Country Park
Longpark
Beansburn
Dean Park
Hillhead
Townholm
Recreation Ground
Balmoral
Ayrshire College
Superstore
Bonnyton
KILMARNOCK West Langlands
To University Hospital Crosshouse
Woodstock St.
The Garage
Portland
Rugby Road
Strawberrybank
Strawberrybank Gardens
Reformers Monument
Burns Monument
Kay Park
Old High Kirk
Nisbet Stone
Burns Mall Cross
Council Offices
Coun. Offs.
St. Marnock St.
Palace Theatre
Sir James Shaw Statue
Dick Institute
London Road
Holehouse Road
Courts
Fowlds St.
New Mill Rd.
Kilmarnock FC
Howard Park
Galleon Leisure Centre
Cinema
Recreation Ground
To Kirklandside Hospital
River Irvine

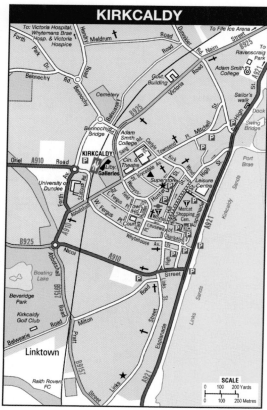

KIRKCALDY

To: Victoria Hospital, Whytemans Brae Hosp. & Victoria Hospice
To Fife Ice Arena
Meldrum
Ravenscraig Park
Bennochy Rd.
Govt. Building
Adam Smith College
Cemetery
Sailor's walk
Dock
Swing Bridge
Port Brae
Bennochy Bridge
Adam Smith College
Oriel A910 Road
KIRKCALDY
Liby. Galleries
Cin. Theatre
University of Dundee
Superstore
Leisure Centre
Mercat Shopping Cen.
Links Sands
Nicol A910 Street
Boating Lake
Beveridge Park
Kirkcaldy Golf Club
Linktown
Balwearie
Raith Rovers FC
Links
Esplanade
Milton
Pratt

SCALE
0 100 200 Yards
0 100 200 Metres

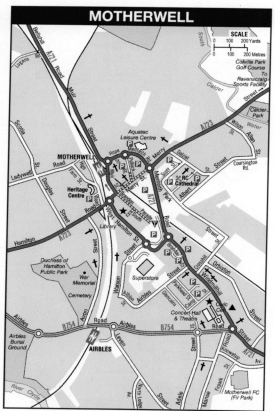

MOTHERWELL

SCALE
0 100 200 Yards
0 100 200 Metres

Colville Park Golf Course
To Ravenscraig Sports Facility
Calder Park
Calder Water
Aquatec Leisure Centre
Coursington Rd.
MOTHERWELL
Heritage Centre
Ladywell
RC Cathedral
Library
Duchess of Hamilton Public Park
War Memorial
Cemetery
Superstore
Hamilton
Concert Hall & Theatre
Civic Centre
Airbles Burial Ground
AIRBLES
Motherwell FC (Fir Park)
River Clyde

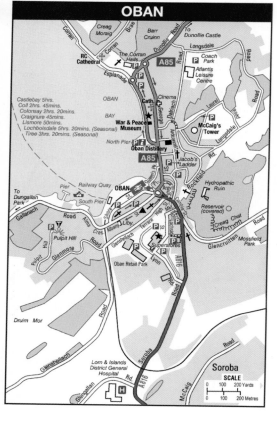

OBAN

Creag Moraig
To Dunollie Castle
Barr Cruinn
Longsdale
RC Cathedral
The Corran Halls
Coach Park
Esplanade
Atlantis Leisure Centre
OBAN BAY
Cath.
Cinema
Castlebay 5hrs.
Coll 2hrs. 45mins.
Colonsay 2hrs. 20mins.
Craignure 45mins.
Lismore 50mins.
Lochboisdale 5hrs. 20mins. (Seasonal)
Tiree 3hrs. 20mins. (Seasonal)
War & Peace Museum
McCaig's Tower
North Pier
Oban Distillery
Jacob's Ladder
Hydropathic Ruin
To Dungallan Park
Pier
Railway Quay
OBAN
Reservoir (covered)
Creag Chat
South Pier
Gallanach
Pulpit Hill
Glenmore
Liby.
Superstores
Mossfield Park
Glencruitten
Oban Retail Park
Druim Mor
Glenshellach
Lorn & Islands District General Hospital
Soroba

SCALE
0 100 200 Yards
0 100 200 Metres

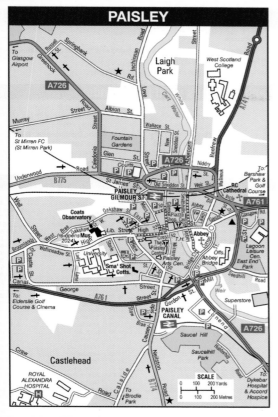

PAISLEY

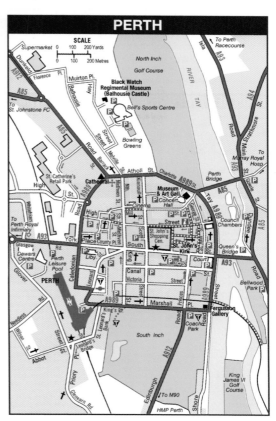

PERTH

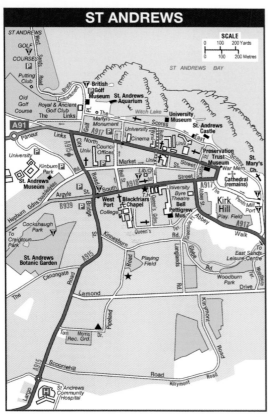

ST ANDREWS

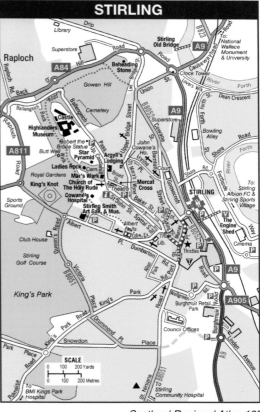

STIRLING

INDEX TO CITIES, TOWNS, VILLAGES, HAMLETS & LOCATIONS

1. A strict alphabetical order is used e.g. An Gleann Ur follows Angerton but precedes Ankerville.
2. The map reference given refers to the actual map square in which the town spot or built-up area is located and not to the place name.
3. Only one reference is given although due to page overlaps the place may appear on more than one page.
4. Where two or more places of the same name occur in the same County or Unitary Authority, the nearest large town is also given; e.g. Achiemore *High*.....1E **87** (nr Durness) indicates that Achiemore is located in square 1E on page **87** and is situated near Durness in the Unitary Authority of Highland.
5. Major towns & destinations are shown in bold i.e. **Aberdeen** *Aber*.....**102** (1E **61**). Where they appear on a Town Plan a second page reference is given.

COUNTIES AND UNITARY AUTHORITIES with the abbreviations used in this index

Aberdeen : *Aber*
Aberdeenshire : *Abers*
Angus : *Ang*
Argyll & Bute : *Arg*
Clackmannanshire : *Clac*
Cumbria : *Cumb*
Dumfries & Galloway : *Dum*
Dundee : *D'dee*
East Ayrshire : *E Ayr*
East Dunbartonshire : *E Dun*
East Lothian : *E Lot*
East Renfrewshire : *E Ren*
Edinburgh : *Edin*
Falkirk : *Falk*
Fife : *Fife*
Glasgow : *Glas*
Highland : *High*
Inverclyde : *Inv*
Midlothian : *Midl*
Moray : *Mor*
North Ayrshire : *N Ayr*
North Lanarkshire : *N Lan*
Northumberland : *Nmbd*
Orkney : *Orkn*
Perth & Kinross : *Per*
Renfrewshire : *Ren*
Scottish Borders : *Bord*
Shetland : *Shet*
South Ayrshire : *S Ayr*
South Lanarkshire : *S Lan*
Stirling : *Stir*
West Dunbartonshire : *W Dun*
West Lothian : *W Lot*
Western Isles : *W Isl*

INDEX

A

Abberwick *Nmbd*....4E **25**
Abbey St Bathans *Bord*....3D **35**
Abbeytown *Cumb*....2A **8**
Aberarder *High*....3D **67**
Aberargie *Per*....2A **42**
Aberchalder *High*....1A **56**
Aberchirder *Abers*....4B **80**
Abercorn *W Lot*....2C **32**
Abercrombie *Fife*....3E **43**
Aberdalgie *Per*....1F **41**
Aberdeen *Aber*....**102** (1E **61**)
Aberdeen International Airport *Aber*....4D **71**
Aberdour *Fife*....1D **33**
Aberfeldy *Per*....3D **49**
Aberfoyle *Stir*....3A **40**
Aberlady *E Lot*....1A **34**
Aberlemno *Ang*....2E **51**
Abernethy *Per*....2A **42**
Abernyte *Per*....4B **50**
Aberuthven *Per*....2E **41**
Abhainn Suidhe *W Isl*....2E **95**
Abington *S Lan*....3E **21**
Aboyne *Abers*....2A **60**
Abriachan *High*....2C **66**
Abronhill *N Lan*....2F **31**
Abune-the-Hill *Orkn*....1A **98**
Acairseid *W Isl*....2C **92**
Acha *Arg*....2G **91**
Achachork *High*....1D **63**
Achadh a' Chuirn *High*....3F **63**
Achahoish *Arg*....2B **28**
Achaleven *Arg*....4A **46**
Achallader *Arg*....3E **47**
Acha Mor *W Isl*....4E **97**
Achanalt *High*....3F **75**
Achandunie *High*....2D **77**
Ach' an Todhair *High*....4D **55**
Achany *High*....3A **84**
Achaphubuil *High*....4D **55**
Acharacle *High*....1D **45**
Acharn *Ang*....4D **59**
Acharn *Per*....3C **48**
Acharole *High*....2B **90**
Achateny *High*....1C **44**
Achavanich *High*....3A **90**
Achdalieu *High*....4D **55**
Achduart *High*....3B **82**
Achentoul *High*....4D **89**
Achfary *High*....4D **87**
Achfrish *High*....2A **84**
Achgarve *High*....1B **74**
Achiemore *High*....1E **87** (nr Durness)
Achiemore *High*....2D **89** (nr Thurso)
A' Chill *High*....1B **52**
Achiltibuie *High*....3B **82**
Achina *High*....1C **88**
Achinahuagh *High*....1A **88**
Achindarroch *High*....2B **46**
Achinduich *High*....3A **84**
Achinduin *Arg*....4F **45**
Achininver *High*....1A **88**
Achintee *High*....1C **64**
Achintraid *High*....2B **64**
Achleck *Arg*....3B **44**
Achlorachan *High*....4A **76**
Achluachrach *High*....3F **55**
Achlyness *High*....2D **87**
Achmelvich *High*....1B **82**
Achmony *High*....2C **66**
Achmore *High*....2B **64** (nr Stromeferry)
Achmore *High*....4B **82** (nr Ullapool)
Achnacarnin *High*....4B **86**
Achnacarry *High*....3E **55**
Achnaclerach *High*....3B **76**
Achnacloich *High*....1E **53**
Ach na Cloiche *High*....1E **53**
Achnaconeran *High*....4B **66**
Achnacroish *Arg*....3F **45**
Achnafalnich *Arg*....1D **39**
Achnagarron *High*....2D **77**
Achnagoul *Arg*....3B **38**
Achnaha *High*....1B **44**
Achnahanat *High*....4A **84**
Achnahannet *High*....3A **68**
Achnairn *High*....2A **84**
Achnamara *Arg*....1B **28**
Achnanellan *High*....3D **55**
Achnasheen *High*....4E **75**
Achnashellach *High*....1D **65**
Achosnich *High*....1B **44**
Achow *High*....4B **90**
Achranich *High*....3E **45**
Achreamie *High*....1F **89**
Achriabhach *High*....1C **46**
Achriesgill *High*....2D **87**
Achrimsdale *High*....3E **85**
Achscrabster *High*....1F **89**
Achtoty *High*....1B **88**
Achuvoldrach *High*....2A **88**
Achvaich *High*....4C **84**
Achvoan *High*....3C **84**
Ackergill *High*....2C **90**
Ackergillshore *High*....2C **90**
Adabroc *W Isl*....1G **97**
Adderstone *Nmbd*....2E **25**
Addiewell *W Lot*....3B **32**
Addinston *Bord*....4B **34**
Advie *High*....2C **68**
Adziel *Abers*....4E **81**
Ae *Dum*....3E **13**
Affleck *Abers*....3D **71**
Affric Lodge *High*....3E **65**
Aglionby *Cumb*....2D **9**
Aiginis *W Isl*....3F **97**
Aikers *Orkn*....3C **98**
Aiketgate *Cumb*....3D **9**
Aikhead *Cumb*....3B **8**
Aikton *Cumb*....2B **8**
Ainstable *Cumb*....3E **9**
Aird *W Isl*....2G **93** (nr Benbecula)
Aird *W Isl*....3G **97** (nr Isle of Lewis)
Aird *High*....2A **74** (nr Port Henderson)
Aird *High*....1E **53** (nr Tarskavaig)
Aird *Arg*....3E **37**
Aird *Dum*....1B **4**
Aird, The *High*....4D **73**
Àird a Bhasair *High*....1F **53**
Aird a Mhachair *W Isl*....3G **93**
Aird a Mhulaidh *W Isl*....1F **95**
Aird Asaig *W Isl*....2F **95**
Aird Dhail *W Isl*....1F **97**
Airdens *High*....4B **84**
Airdeny *Arg*....1A **38**
Aird Mhidhinis *W Isl*....2C **92**
Aird Mhighe *W Isl*....3F **95** (nr Ceann a Bhaigh)
Aird Mhighe *W Isl*....4E **95** (nr Fionnsabhagh)
Aird Mhor *W Isl*....2C **92** (nr Barra)
Aird Mhor *W Isl*....3H **93** (nr South Uist)
Airdrie *N Lan*....3F **31**
Aird Shleibhe *W Isl*....4F **95**
Aird Thunga *W Isl*....3F **97**
Aird Uig *W Isl*....3B **96**
Airidh a Bhruaich *W Isl*....1G **95**
Airies *Dum*....1A **4**
Airntully *Per*....4F **49**
Airor *High*....1A **54**
Airth *Falk*....1B **32**
Aisgernis *W Isl*....5G **93**
Aith *Shet*....3H **101** (nr Fetlar)
Aith *Shet*....1B **100** (nr Mainland)
Aithsetter *Shet*....3C **100**
Akeld *Nmbd*....3C **24**
Albyfield *Cumb*....2E **9**
Alcaig *High*....4C **76**
Aldclune *Per*....1E **49**
Aldochlay *Arg*....4E **39**
Aldoth *Cumb*....3A **8**
Alexandria *W Dun*....1B **30**
Alford *Abers*....4A **70**
Aline Lodge *W Isl*....1F **95**
Alladale Lodge *High*....1B **76**
Allanbank *N Lan*....4A **32**
Allanton *Bord*....4E **35**
Allanton *N Lan*....4A **32**
Allerby *Cumb*....4F **7**
Alligin Shuas *High*....4B **74**
Alloa *Clac*....4D **41**
Allonby *Cumb*....3F **7**
Alloway *S Ayr*....4E **19**
Alltgobhlach *N Ayr*....1F **17**
Alltnacaillich *High*....3F **87**
Allt na h' Airbhe *High*....4C **82**
Alltour *High*....3F **55**
Alltsigh *High*....4B **66**
Almondbank *Per*....1F **41**
Alness *High*....3D **77**
Alnessferry *High*....3D **77**
Alnham *Nmbd*....4C **24**
Alnmouth *Nmbd*....4F **25**
Alnwick *Nmbd*....4E **25**
Alston *Cumb*....3F **9**
Altandhu *High*....2A **82**
Altanduin *High*....1D **85**
Altass *High*....3F **83**
Alterwall *High*....1B **90**
Altgaltraig *Arg*....2E **29**
Altnabreac *High*....3F **89**
Altnacealgach *High*....2D **83**
Altnafeadh *High*....2D **47**
Altnaharra *High*....4A **88**
Altonhill *E Ayr*....2F **19**
Altrua *High*....2F **55**
Alva *Clac*....4D **41**
Alves *Mor*....3C **78**
Alvie *High*....1F **57**
Alwinton *Nmbd*....4C **24**
Alyth *Per*....3B **50**
Amatnatua *High*....4F **83**
Am Baile *W Isl*....1C **92**
Amble *Nmbd*....4F **25**
Amisfield *Dum*....3F **13**
Amulree *Per*....4E **49**
Anaheilt *High*....1F **45**
An Àird *High*....1E **53**
An Camus Darach *High*....2F **53**
An Cnoc *W Isl*....3F **97**
An Cnoc Ard *W Isl*....1G **97**
An Coroghon *High*....1B **52**
Ancroft *Nmbd*....1D **25**
Ancrum *Bord*....3F **23**
An Dùnan *High*....3E **63**
Angerton *Cumb*....2B **8**
An Gleann Ur *W Isl*....3F **97**
Ankerville *High*....2F **77**
An Leth Meadhanach *W Isl*....1C **92**
Annan *Dum*....1B **8**
Annat *Arg*....1B **38**
Annat *High*....4B **74**
Annathill *N Lan*....2F **31**
Annbank *S Ayr*....3F **19**
An Sailean *High*....1D **45**
Anston *S Lan*....1F **21**
Anstruther Easter *Fife*....3E **43**
Anstruther Wester *Fife*....3E **43**
An Taobh Tuath *W Isl*....4D **94**
An t-Aodann Ban *High*....4C **72**
An t Ath Leathann *High*....3F **63**
An Teanga *High*....1F **53**
Anthorn *Cumb*....2A **8**
An t-Ob *W Isl*....4E **95**
An t-Òrd *High*....4F **63**
Anwoth *Dum*....2A **6**
Appin *Arg*....3A **46**
Applecross *High*....1A **64**
Applegarthtown *Dum*....3A **14**
Applethwaite *Cumb*....4B **8**
Appletreehall *Bord*....4E **23**
Arabella *High*....2F **77**
Arasaig *High*....3F **53**
Arbeadie *Abers*....2B **60**
Arbirlot *Ang*....3F **51**
Arbroath *Ang*....3F **51**
Arbuthnott *Abers*....4D **61**
Arcan *High*....4C **76**
Archargary *High*....2C **88**
Archiestown *Mor*....1D **69**
Ardachu *High*....3B **84**
Ardalanish *Arg*....2A **36**
Ardaneaskan *High*....2B **64**
Ardarroch *High*....2B **64**
Ardbeg *Arg*....1F **29** (nr Dunoon)
Ardbeg *Arg*....1B **16** (nr Islay)
Ardbeg *Arg*....3E **29** (nr Isle of Bute)
Ardcharnich *High*....1E **75**
Ardchiavaig *Arg*....2A **36**
Ardchonnell *Arg*....2A **38**
Ardchrishnish *Arg*....1B **36**
Ardchronie *High*....1D **77**
Ardchullarie *Stir*....2A **40**
Ardchyle *Stir*....1A **40**
Ard-dhubh *High*....1A **64**
Ardechive *High*....2E **55**
Ardelve *High*....3B **64**
Arden *Arg*....1B **30**
Ardendrain *High*....2C **66**
Ardentinny *Arg*....1F **29**
Ardeonaig *Stir*....4B **48**
Ardersier *High*....4E **77**
Ardery *High*....1E **45**
Ardessie *High*....1D **75**
Ardfern *Arg*....3F **37**
Ardfernal *Arg*....2F **27**
Ardfin *Arg*....3E **27**
Ardgartan *Arg*....3D **39**
Ardgay *High*....4B **84**
Ardgour *High*....1B **46**
Ardheslaig *High*....4A **74**
Ardindrean *High*....1E **75**
Ardlamont House *Arg*....3D **29**
Ardler *Per*....3B **50**
Ardlui *Arg*....2E **39**
Ardlussa *Arg*....1A **28**
Ardmair *High*....4C **82**
Ardmay *Arg*....3D **39**
Ardminish *Arg*....1D **17**
Ardmolich *High*....4A **54**
Ardmore *High*....2D **87** (nr Kinlochbervie)
Ardmore *High*....1E **77** (nr Tain)
Ardnacross *Arg*....3C **44**
Ardnadam *Arg*....1F **29**
Ardnagrask *High*....1C **66**
Ardnamurach *High*....2B **54**
Ardnarff *High*....2B **64**
Ardnastang *High*....1F **45**
Ardoch *Per*....4F **49**
Ardochy House *High*....1F **55**
Ardpatrick *Arg*....3B **28**
Ardrishaig *Arg*....1C **28**
Ardroag *High*....1B **62**
Ardross *High*....2D **77**
Ardrossan *N Ayr*....1D **19**
Ardshealach *High*....1D **45**
Ardslignish *High*....1C **44**
Ardtalla *Arg*....4E **27**
Ardtalnaig *Per*....4C **48**
Ardtoe *High*....4F **53**
Arduaine *Arg*....2E **37**
Ardullie *High*....3C **76**
Ardvasar *High*....1F **53**
Ardvorlich *Per*....1B **40**
Ardwell *Dum*....3C **4**
Ardwell *Mor*....2E **69**
Arean *High*....4F **53**
Aridhglas *Arg*....1A **36**
Arinacrinachd *High*....4A **74**
Arinagour *Arg*....2H **91**
Arisaig *High*....3F **53**
Ariundle *High*....1F **45**
Arivegaig *High*....1D **45**
Armadail *High*....1F **53**
Armadale *High*....1F **53** (nr Isleornsay)
Armadale *High*....1C **88** (nr Strathy)
Armadale *W Lot*....3B **32**
Armathwaite *Cumb*....3E **9**
Arncroach *Fife*....3E **43**
Arnicle *Arg*....2E **17**
Arnisdale *High*....4B **64**
Arnish *High*....1E **63**
Arniston *Midl*....3F **33**
Arnol *W Isl*....2E **97**
Arnprior *Stir*....4B **40**
Aros Mains *Arg*....3C **44**
Arpafeelie *High*....4D **77**
Arrochar *Arg*....3D **39**
Arscaig *High*....2A **84**
Artafallie *High*....1D **67**
Arthrath *Abers*....2E **71**
Arthurstone *Per*....3B **50**
Ascog *Arg*....3F **29**
Ashfield *Stir*....3C **40**
Ashgill *S Lan*....1C **20**
Ashgrove *Mor*....3D **79**
Ashkirk *Bord*....3D **23**
Ashton *Inv*....2A **30**
Askham *Cumb*....4E **9**
Aspatria *Cumb*....3A **8**
Astle *High*....4C **84**
Athelstaneford *E Lot*....2B **34**
Ath-Tharracail *High*....1D **45**
Attadale *High*....2C **64**
Auchamie *Abers*....1B **70**
Auchattie *Abers*....2B **60**
Auchavan *Ang*....1A **50**
Auchbreck *Mor*....3D **69**
Auchenback *E Ren*....4D **31**
Auchenblae *Abers*....4C **60**
Auchenbrack *Dum*....2C **12**
Auchenbreck *Arg*....1E **29**
Auchencairn *Dum*....2C **6** (nr Dalbeattie)
Auchencairn *Dum*....3E **13** (nr Dumfries)
Auchencarroch *W Dun*....1C **30**
Auchencrow *Bord*....3E **35**
Auchendennan *Arg*....1B **30**
Auchendinny *Midl*....3E **33**
Auchengray *S Lan*....4B **32**
Auchenhalrig *Mor*....3E **79**
Auchenheath *S Lan*....1D **21**
Auchenlochan *Arg*....2D **29**
Auchenmade *N Ayr*....1E **19**
Auchenmalg *Dum*....2D **5**
Auchentiber *N Ayr*....1E **19**
Auchenvennel *Arg*....1A **30**
Auchindrain *Arg*....3B **38**
Auchininna *Abers*....1B **70**
Auchinleck *Dum*....4F **11**
Auchinleck *E Ayr*....3A **20**
Auchinloch *N Lan*....2E **31**
Auchinstarry *N Lan*....2F **31**
Auchleven *Abers*....3B **70**
Auchlochan *S Lan*....2D **21**
Auchlunachan *High*....1E **75**
Auchmillan *E Ayr*....3A **20**
Auchmithie *Ang*....3F **51**
Auchmuirbridge *Fife*....3B **42**
Auchmull *Ang*....4A **60**
Auchnacree *Ang*....1D **51**
Auchnafree *Per*....4D **49**
Auchnagallin *High*....2B **68**
Auchnagatt *Abers*....1E **71**
Aucholzie *Abers*....2E **59**
Auchreddie *Abers*....1D **71**
Auchterarder *Per*....2E **41**
Auchteraw *High*....1A **56**
Auchterderran *Fife*....4B **42**
Auchterhouse *Ang*....4C **50**
Auchtermuchty *Fife*....2B **42**
Auchterneed *High*....4B **76**
Auchtertool *Fife*....4B **42**
Auchtertyre *High*....3B **64**
Auchtubh *Stir*....1A **40**
Auckengill *High*....1C **90**
Auds *Abers*....3B **80**
Aughertree *Cumb*....4B **8**
Auldearn *High*....4A **78**

Auldgirth – Bragar

Auldgirth Dum 3E 13
Auldhouse S Lan 4E 31
Ault a' chruinn High 3C 64
Aultbea High 1B 74
Aultdearg High 3F 75
Aultgrishan High 1A 74
Aultguish Inn High 2A 76
Aultibea High 1F 85
Aultiphurst High 1D 89
Aultivullin High 1D 89
Aultmore Mor 4F 79
Aultnamain Inn High 1D 77
Avielochan High 4A 68
Aviemore High 102 (4F 67)
Avoch High 4E 77
Avonbridge Falk 2B 32
Ayle Nmbd 3F 9
Ayr S Ayr 103 (3E 19)
Ayres of Selivoe Shet 2A 100
Ayton Bord 3F 35
Aywick Shet 3H 101

B

Bac W Isl 2F 97
Backaland Orkn 4G 99
Backaskaill Orkn 2F 99
Backfolds Abers 4F 81
Backhill Abers 2C 70
Backhill of Clackriach Abers 1E 71
Backies High 3D 85
Backmuir of New Gilston Fife 3D 43
Back of Keppoch High 3F 53
Badachonacher High 2D 77
Badachro High 2A 74
Badanloch Lodge High 4C 88
Badavanich High 4E 75
Badcall High 2D 87
Badcaul High 4B 82
Baddidarach High 1B 82
Baddoch Abers 3C 58
Badenscallie High 3B 82
Badenscoth Abers 2C 70
Badentarbat High 2B 82
Badicaul High 3A 64
Badlipster High 3B 90
Badluarach High 4A 82
Badnaban High 1B 82
Badnabay High 3D 87
Badnagie High 4A 90
Badnellan High 3D 85
Badninish High 4C 84
Badrallach High 4B 82
Bàgh a Chàise W Isl 5D 94
Bàgh a' Chaisteil W Isl 3B 92
Baghasdal W Isl 1C 92
Bagh Mor W Isl 2H 93
Bagh Shiarabhagh W Isl 2C 92
Baile W Isl 4D 94
Baile Ailein W Isl 4D 96
Baile an Truiseil W Isl 1E 97
Baile Boidheach Arg 2B 28
Baile Glas W Isl 2H 93
Bailemeonach Arg 3D 45
Baile Mhanaich W Isl 2G 93
Baile Mhartainn W Isl 5B 94
Baile MhicPhail W Isl 5C 94
Baile Mor W Isl 1G 93
Baile Mór Arg 5H 91
Baile nan Cailleach W Isl 2G 93
Baile Raghaill W Isl 1G 93
Baileyhead Cumb 3E 15
Bailiesward Abers 2F 69
Bail' lochdrach W Isl 2H 93
Baillieston Glas 3E 31
Bail Uachdraich W Isl 1H 93
Bail' Ur Tholastaidh W Isl 2G 97
Bainsford Falk 1A 32
Bainshole Abers 2B 70
Baintown Fife 3C 42
Balachuirn High 1E 63
Balbeg High 2B 66
(nr Cannich)
Balbeg High 3B 66
(nr Loch Ness)
Balbeggie Per 1A 42
Balblair High 4A 84
(nr Bonar Bridge)
Balblair High 3E 77
(nr Invergordon)
Balblair High 1C 66
(nr Inverness)
Balcathie Ang 4F 51
Balchladich High 4B 86
Balchraggan High 1C 66
Balchrick High 2C 86
Balcurvie Fife 3C 42
Baldinnie Fife 2D 43
Baldwinholme Cumb 2C 8
Balearn Abers 4E 81
Balemartine Arg 3E 91
Balephetrish Arg 3F 91
Balephuil Arg 3E 91
Balerno Edin 3D 33
Balevullin Arg 3E 91
Balfield Ang 1E 51
Balfour Orkn 1C 98
Balfron Stir 1D 31
Balgaveny Abers 1B 70
Balgonar Fife 4F 41
Balgowan High 2D 57
Balgown High 3C 72
Balgrochan E Dun 2E 31
Balgy High 4B 74
Balhalgardy Abers 3C 70
Baliasta Shet 1H 101
Baligill High 1D 89
Balintore Ang 2B 50
Balintore High 2F 77
Balintraid High 2E 77
Balkeerie Ang 3C 50
Ballachulish High 2B 46
Ballantrae S Ayr 3B 10
Ballater Abers 2E 59
Ballencrieff E Lot 2A 34
Ballencrieff Toll W Lot 2B 32
Ballentoul Per 1D 49
Balliemore Arg 1E 29
(nr Dunoon)
Balliemore Arg 1F 37
(nr Oban)
Ballieward High 2B 68
Ballimore Stir 2A 40
Ballingry Fife 4A 42
Ballinluig Per 2E 49
Ballintuim Per 2A 50
Balliveolan Arg 3F 45
Balloan High 3A 84
Balloch High 1E 67
Balloch N Lan 2F 31
Balloch Per 2D 41
Balloch W Dun 1B 30
Ballochan Abers 2A 60
Ballochgoy Arg 3E 29
Ballochmyle E Ayr 3A 20
Ballochroy Arg 4B 28
Ballygown Arg 3B 44
Ballygrant Arg 3D 27
Ballymichael N Ayr 2A 18
Balmacara High 3B 64
Balmaclellan Dum 4B 12
Balmacqueen High 2D 73
Balmaha Stir 4F 39
Balmalcolm Fife 3C 42
Balmalloch N Lan 2F 31
Balmeanach High 2E 63
Balmedie Abers 4E 71
Balmerino Fife 1C 42
Balmore E Dun 2E 31
Balmore High 1B 62
Balmullo Fife 1D 43
Balmurrie Dum 1D 5
Balnaboth Ang 1C 50
Balnabruaich High 2E 77
Balnabruich High 1F 85
Balnacoil High 2D 85
Balnacra High 1C 64
Balnacroft Abers 2D 59
Balnageith Mor 4B 78
Balnaglaic High 2B 66
Balnagrantach High 2B 66
Balnaguard Per 2E 49
Balnahard Arg 4B 36
Balnain High 2B 66
Balnakeil High 1E 87
Balnaknock High 3D 73
Balnamoon Abers 4E 81
Balnamoon Ang 1E 51
Balnapaling High 3E 77
Balornock Glas 3E 31
Balquhidder Stir 1A 40
Baltasound Shet 1H 101
Baltersan Dum 1F 5
Balthangie Abers 4D 81
Balvaird High 4C 76
Balvaird Per 2A 42
Balvenie Mor 1E 69
Balvicar Arg 2E 37
Balvraid High 4B 64
Balvraid Lodge High 2F 67
Bamburgh Nmbd 2E 25
Banavie High 4E 55
Banchory Abers 2B 60
Banchory-Devenick Abers 1E 61
Banff Abers 3B 80
Bankend Dum 1F 7
Bankfoot Per 4F 49
Bankglen E Ayr 4B 20
Bankhead Aber 4D 71
Bankhead Abers 1B 60
Bankhead S Lan 1D 21
Banknock Falk 2F 31
Banks Cumb 1E 9
Bankshill Dum 3A 14
Banniskirk High 2A 90
Bannockburn Stir 4D 41
Banton N Lan 2F 31
Barabhas W Isl 1E 97
Barabhas Iarach W Isl 2E 97
Baramore High 4F 53
Barassie S Ayr 2E 19
Baravullin Arg 3A 46
Barbaraville High 2E 77
Barbhas Uarach W Isl 1E 97
Barbieston S Ayr 4F 19
Barcaldine Arg 3A 46
Barclose Cumb 1D 9
Bardister Shet 4F 101
Bardnabeinne High 4C 84
Bardowie E Dun 2D 31
Bardrainney Inv 2B 30
Barelees Nmbd 2B 24
Bargeddie N Lan 3E 31
Bargrennan Dum 4E 11
Barharrow Dum 2B 6
Barlanark Glas 3E 31
Barmoor Nmbd 2D 25
Barmulloch Glas 3E 31
Barnbarroch Dum 2D 7
Barnhead Ang 2F 51
Barnhill D'dee 4D 51
Barnhill Mor 4C 78
Barnhill Per 1A 42
Barnhills Dum 4A 10
Barony, The Orkn 1A 98
Barr Dum 1C 12
Barr S Ayr 2D 11
Barra Airport W Isl 2B 92
Barrachan Dum 3E 5
Barraglom W Isl 3C 96
Barrahormid Arg 1B 28
Barrapol Arg 3E 91
Barravullin Arg 3F 37
Barrhead E Ren 4D 31
Barrhill S Ayr 3D 11
Barrmill N Ayr 4B 30
Barrock High 5A 98
Barrowburn Nmbd 4B 24
Barry Ang 4E 51
Barthol Chapel Abers 2D 71
Barton Cumb 4D 9
Bassendean Bord 1F 23
Bassenthwaite Cumb 4B 8
Basta Shet 2H 101
Bathgate W Lot 3B 32
Bathville W Lot 3B 32
Bauds of Cullen Mor 3F 79
Baugh Arg 3F 91
Bay High 4B 72
Bayles Cumb 3F 9
Beacrabhaic W Isl 3F 95
Beadnell Nmbd 3F 25
Beal Nmbd 1D 25
Beanley Nmbd 4D 25
Beaquoy Orkn 5E 99
Bearsden E Dun 2D 31
Beattock Dum 1F 13
Beauly High 1C 66
Beaumont Cumb 2C 8
Beckfoot Cumb 3F 7
Bedrule Bord 4F 23
Beeswing Dum 1D 7
Beinn Casgro W Isl 4F 97
Beith N Ayr 4B 30
Belfatton Abers 4F 81
Belford Nmbd 2E 25
Belhaven E Lot 2C 34
Belhelvie Abers 4E 71
Belhinnie Abers 3F 69
Bellabeg Abers 4E 69
Belladrum High 1C 66
Bellamore S Ayr 3D 11
Bellanoch Arg 4F 37
Belleheiglash Mor 2C 68
Belle Vue Cumb 4A 8
Bellfield S Lan 2D 21
Belliehill Ang 1E 51
Bellochantuy Arg 2D 17
Bellsbank E Ayr 1F 11
Bellshill N Lan 4F 31
Bellshill Nmbd 2E 25
Bellside N Lan 4A 32
Bellspool Bord 2A 22
Bellsquarry W Lot 3C 32
Belmaduthy High 4D 77
Belmont S Ayr 3E 19
Belmont Shet 1H 101
Belnacraig Abers 4E 69
Belston S Ayr 3E 19
Belts of Collonach Abers 2B 60
Bemersyde Bord 2D 23
Ben Alder Lodge High 4C 56
Ben Armine Lodge High 2C 84
Benbecula Airport W Isl 2G 93
Benbuie Dum 2C 12
Benderloch Arg 4A 46
Bendronaig Lodge High 2D 65
Benholm Abers 4D 61
Benmore Lodge High 2E 83
Bennecarrigan N Ayr 3A 18
Bennethead Cumb 4D 9
Benston Shet 1C 100
Benstonhall Orkn 4G 99
Bent Abers 4B 60
Bentpath Dum 2C 14
Bents W Lot 3B 32
Benvie D'dee 4C 50
Beoraidbeg High 2F 53
Bernera High 3B 64
Bernice Arg 4C 38
Bernisdale High 4D 73
Berriedale High 1F 85
Berrier Cumb 4C 8
Berrington Nmbd 1D 25
Berrington Law Nmbd 1C 24
Berryhillock Mor 3A 80
Berryscaur Dum 2A 14
Berwick-upon-Tweed Nmbd 4F 35
Bettyhill High 1C 88
Beul an Atha Arg 3D 27
Bewaldeth Cumb 4B 8
Bewcastle Cumb 4E 15
Bhalton W Isl 3B 96
Bhatarsaigh W Isl 3B 92
Biddlestone Nmbd 4C 24
Bieldside Aber 1D 61
Biggar S Lan 2F 21
Bighouse High 1D 89
Biglands Cumb 2B 8
Big Sand High 2A 74
Bigton Shet 4B 100
Bilbster High 2B 90
Bilston Midl 3E 33
Bilton Nmbd 4F 25
Bimbister Orkn 1B 98
Bindal High 1A 78
Binniehill Falk 2A 32
Birchburn N Ayr 3A 18
Birchview Mor 2C 68
Birdston E Dun 2E 31
Birgham Bord 2A 24
Birichen High 4C 84
Birkby Cumb 4F 7
Birkenhills Abers 1C 70
Birkenshaw N Lan 3E 31
Birkhall Abers 2E 59
Birkhill Ang 4C 50
Birling Nmbd 4F 25
Birnam Per 3F 49
Birse Abers 2A 60
Birsemore Abers 2A 60
Bishopbriggs E Dun 2E 31
Bishopmill Mor 3D 79
Bishopton Dum 3F 5
Bishopton Ren 2C 30
Bixter Shet 1B 100
Blackburn Abers 4D 71
Blackburn W Lot 3B 32
Black Clauchrie S Ayr 3D 11
Black Corries High 2D 47
Black Crofts Arg 4A 46
Blackdog Abers 4E 71
Blackdyke Cumb 2A 8
Blackford Cumb 1C 8
Blackford Per 3D 41
Blackhall Edin 2E 33
Blackhall Ren 3C 30
Blackhill Abers 1F 71
Blackhill High 4C 72
Blackhills Abers 3E 81
Blackhills High 4A 78
Blacklunans Per 1A 50
Black Mount Arg 3D 47
Blackness Falk 2C 32
Blackpool Gate Cumb 4E 15
Blackridge W Lot 3A 32
Blackrock Arg 3D 27
Blackshaw Dum 1F 7
Blacktop Aber 1D 61
Blackwaterfoot N Ayr 3F 17
Blackwood Dum 3E 13
Blackwood S Lan 1C 20
Bladnoch Dum 2F 5
Blagill Cumb 3F 9
Blaich High 4D 55
Blain High 1D 45
Blair Atholl Per 1D 49
Blair Drummond Stir 4C 40
Blairgowrie Per 3A 50
Blairhall Fife 1C 32
Blairingone Per 4E 41
Blairlogie Stir 4D 41
Blairmore Abers 2F 69
Blairmore Arg 1F 29
Blairmore High 2C 86
Blairquhanan W Dun 1C 30
Blandy High 1B 88
Blanefield Stir 2D 31
Blantyre S Lan 4E 31
Blarmachfoldach High 1B 46
Blarnalearoch High 4C 82
Blathaisbhal W Isl 5C 94
Blebocraigs Fife 2D 43
Blencarn Cumb 4F 9
Blencogo Cumb 3A 8
Blennerhasset Cumb 3A 8
Blindburn Nmbd 4B 24
Blindcrake Cumb 4A 8
Blitterlees Cumb 2A 8
Bloomfield Bord 3E 23
Blyth Bord 1A 22
Blyth Bank Bord 1A 22
Blyth Bridge Bord 1A 22
Boarhills Fife 2E 43
Boath High 2C 76
Boat of Garten High 4A 68
Boddam Abers 1F 71
Boddam Shet 5B 100
Bogallan High 4D 77
Bogbrae Croft Abers 2F 71
Bogend S Ayr 2E 19
Boghall Midl 3E 33
Boghall W Lot 3B 32
Boghead S Lan 1C 20
Bogindollo Ang 2D 51
Bogmoor Mor 3E 79
Bogniebrae Abers 1A 70
Bograxie Abers 4C 70
Bogside N Lan 4A 32
Bogton Abers 4B 80
Bogue Dum 3B 12
Bohenie High 3F 55
Boirseam W Isl 4E 95
Boleside Bord 2D 23
Bolshan Ang 2F 51
Boltachan Per 2D 49
Bolton E Lot 2B 34
Bolton Nmbd 4E 25
Boltonfellend Cumb 1D 9
Boltongate Cumb 3B 8
Bolton Low Houses Cumb 3B 8
Bolton New Houses Cumb 3B 8
Bolton Wood Lane Cumb 3B 8
Bonar Bridge High 4B 84
Bonawe Arg 4B 46
Bonchester Bridge Bord 4E 23
Bo'ness Falk 1B 32
Bonhill W Dun 2B 30
Bonjedward Bord 3F 23
Bonkle N Lan 4A 32
Bonnington Ang 4E 51
Bonnington Edin 3D 33
Bonnybank Fife 3C 42
Bonnybridge Falk 1A 32
Bonnykelly Abers 4D 81
Bonnyrigg Midl 3F 33
Bonnyton Ang 4C 50
Bonnytown Fife 2E 43
Booth of Toft Shet 4G 101
Boquhan Stir 1D 31
Bordlands Bord 1A 22
Boreland Dum 2A 14
Borestone Brae Stir 4C 40
Borgh W Isl 2B 92
(nr Barra)
Borgh W Isl 2G 93
(nr Benbecula)
Borgh W Isl 4D 94
(nr Berneray)
Borgh W Isl 1F 97
(nr Isle of Lewis)
Borghasdal W Isl 4E 95
Borghastan W Isl 2C 96
Borgh na Sgiotaig High 2C 72
Borgie High 2B 88
Borgue Dum 3B 6
Borgue High 1F 85
Borlum High 3C 66
Bornais W Isl 5G 93
Bornesketaig High 2C 72
Borreraig High 4A 72
Borrobol Lodge High 1D 85
Borrodale High 1A 62
Borrowston High 3C 90
Borrowstonehill Orkn 2C 98
Borrowstoun Falk 1B 32
Borthwick Midl 4F 33
Borve High 1D 63
Bostadh W Isl 2C 96
Bothel Cumb 4A 8
Bothwell S Lan 4F 31
Bottacks High 3B 76
Bottomcraig Fife 1C 42
Boulmer Nmbd 4F 25
Bousd Arg 1H 91
Bousta Shet 1A 100
Boustead Hill Cumb 2B 8
Bowden Bord 2E 23
Bower Nmbd 3F 15
Bowermadden High 1B 90
Bowershall Fife 4F 41
Bowertower High 1B 90
Bowhousebog N Lan 4A 32
Bowling W Dun 2C 30
Bowmore Arg 4D 27
Bowness-on-Solway Cumb 1B 8
Bow of Fife Fife 2C 42
Bowriefauld Ang 3E 51
Bowscale Cumb 4C 8
Bowsden Nmbd 1C 24
Bowside Lodge High 1D 89
Boyndie Abers 3B 80
Braal Castle High 2A 90
Brabster High 1C 90
Bracadale High 2C 62
Bracara High 2A 54
Brackenlands Cumb 3B 8
Brackenthwaite Cumb 3B 8
Brackla High 4F 77
Brackletter High 3E 55
Brackloch High 1C 82
Braco Per 3D 41
Bracobrae Mor 4A 80
Bradford Nmbd 2E 25
Brae High 1B 74
Brae Shet 5F 101
Braeantra High 2C 76
Braefield High 2B 66
Braefindon High 4D 77
Braegrum Per 1F 41
Braehead S Lan 2D 21
(nr Coalburn)
Braehead S Lan 4B 32
(nr Forth)
Braehead Ang 2F 51
Braehead Dum 2F 5
Braehead Mor 1D 69
Braehead Orkn 3F 99
Braehoulland Shet 4E 101
Braemar Abers 2C 58
Braemore High 4F 89
(nr Dunbeath)
Braemore High 2E 75
(nr Ullapool)
Brae of Achnahaird High 2B 82
Brae Roy Lodge High 2A 56
Braeside Abers 2E 71
Braeside Inv 2A 30
Braes of Coul Ang 2B 50
Braeswick Orkn 4H 99
Braetongue High 2A 88
Braeval Stir 3A 40
Braevallich Arg 3A 38
Braewick Shet 1B 100
Bragar W Isl 2D 96

Clachaig – Dalston

Clachaig *Arg* 1F 29
Clachamish *High* 4C 72
Clachan *Arg* 4B 28
(nr Kintyre)
Clachan *Arg* 3F 45
(nr Lismore)
Clachan *High* 1C 88
(nr Bettyhill)
Clachan *High* 2E 63
(nr Raasay)
Clachan *High* 3D 73
(nr Staffin)
Clachan *High* 2D 73
(nr Uig)
Clachan Farm *Arg* 2C 38
Clachan na Luib *W Isl* 1H 93
Clachan of Campsie *E Dun* 2E 31
Clachan of Glendaruel *Arg* 1D 29
Clachan-Seil *Arg* 2E 37
Clachan Shannda *W Isl* 5C 94
Clachan Strachur *Arg* 3B 38
Clachbreck *Arg* 2B 28
Clachnaharry *High* 1D 67
Clachtoll *High* 1B 82
Clackmannan *Clac* 4E 41
Clackmarras *Mor* 4D 79
Cladach a Chaolais *W Isl* 1G 93
Cladach Chairinis *W Isl* 2H 93
Cladach Chirceboist *W Isl* 1G 93
Cladach Iolaraigh *W Isl* 1G 93
Cladich *Arg* 1B 38
Claggan *High* 4E 55
(nr Fort William)
Claggan *High* 2E 45
(nr Lochaline)
Claigan *High* 4B 72
Claonaig *Arg* 4C 28
Clappers *Bord* 4F 35
Clapphoull *Shet* 4C 100
Clarebrand *Dum* 1C 6
Clarencefield *Dum* 1F 7
Clarilaw *Bord* 4E 23
Clarkston *E Ren* 4D 31
Clasheddy *High* 1B 88
Clashindarroch *Abers* 2F 69
Clashmore *High* 1E 77
(nr Dornoch)
Clashmore *High* 4B 86
(nr Stoer)
Clashnessie *High* 4B 86
Clashnoir *Mor* 3D 69
Clate *Shet* 5H 101
Clathick *Per* 1D 41
Clathy *Per* 2E 41
Clatt *Abers* 3A 70
Claygate *Dum* 4C 14
Clayholes *Ang* 4E 51
Clayock *High* 2A 90
Cleadale *High* 3D 53
Cleat *Orkn* 3F 99
(nr Braehead)
Cleat *Orkn* 4C 98
(nr St Margaret's Hope)
Cleekhimin *N Lan* 4F 31
Cleigh *Arg* 1F 37
Cleish *Per* 4F 41
Cleland *N Lan* 4A 32
Clennell *Nmbd* 4C 24
Clephanton *High* 4F 77
Clerkhill *High* 1C 88
Clestrain *Orkn* 2B 98
Claid *W Isl* 2B 92
Cliasmol *W Isl* 2E 95
Clibberswick *Shet* 1H 101
Cliburn *Cumb* 4E 9
Cliffburn *Ang* 3F 51
Clifton *Cumb* 4E 9
Clifton *Stir* 4E 47
Climpy *S Lan* 4B 32
Clintmains *Bord* 2F 23
Cliobh *W Isl* 3B 96
Cliuthar *W Isl* 3F 95
Clivocast *Shet* 1H 101
Clochan *Mor* 3F 79
Clochforbie *Abers* 4D 81
Cloddymoss *Mor* 3A 78
Clola *Abers* 1F 71
Closeburn *Dum* 2D 13
Clousta *Shet* 1B 100
Clouston *Orkn* 1A 98
Clova *Abers* 3F 69
Clova *Ang* 4E 59
Clovenfords *Bord* 2D 23
Clovenstone *Abers* 4C 70
Clovullin *High* 1B 46
Cluanie Inn *High* 4D 65
Cluanie Lodge *High* 4D 65
Clunas *High* 1F 67
Clune *High* 3E 67
Clunes *High* 3F 55
Clunie *Per* 3A 50
Cluny *Fife* 4B 42
Clydebank *W Dun* 3D 31
Clynder *Arg* 1A 30
Clynelish *High* 3D 85
Clyth *High* 4B 90
Cnip *W Isl* 3B 96
Cnoc Amhlaigh *W Isl* 3G 97
Coalburn *S Lan* 2D 21
Coalford *Abers* 2D 61
Coalhall *E Ayr* 4F 19
Coalsnaughton *Clac* 4E 41
Coaltown of Balgonie *Fife* 4C 42
Coaltown of Wemyss *Fife* 4C 42
Coanwood *Nmbd* 2F 9
Coatbridge *N Lan* 3F 31
Coatdyke *N Lan* 3F 31
Cock Bridge *Abers* 1D 59
Cockburnspath *Bord* 2D 35
Cockenzie and Port Seton
E Lot 2A 34
Cockermouth *Cumb* 4A 8
Cocklaw *Abers* 1F 71
Cockmuir *Abers* 4E 81
Coignafearn Lodge *High* 4D 67
Coig Peighinnean *W Isl* 1G 97
Coig Peighinnean Bhuirgh
W Isl 1F 97
Coilleag *W Isl* 1C 92
Coillemore *High* 2D 77
Coillore *High* 2C 62
Coire an Fhuarain *W Isl* 3D 96
Col *W Isl* 2F 97
Colaboll *High* 2A 84
Colbost *High* 1B 62
Coldbackie *High* 2B 88
Coldingham *Bord* 3F 35
Coldrain *Per* 3F 41
Coldstream *Bord* 1B 24
Coldwells *Abers* 2F 71
Coldwells Croft *Abers* 3A 70
Cole *Shet* 5F 101
Coleburn *Mor* 4D 79
Colinsburgh *Fife* 3D 43
Colinton *Edin* 3E 33
Colintraive *Arg* 2E 29
Collace *Per* 4B 50
Collam *W Isl* 3F 95
College of Roseisle *Mor* 3C 78
Collessie *Fife* 2B 42
Collieston *Abers* 3F 71
Collin *Dum* 4F 13
Colliston *Ang* 3F 51
Collydean *Fife* 3B 42
Colmonell *S Ayr* 3C 10
Colpy *Abers* 2B 70
Colstoun House *E Lot* 2B 34
Coltfield *Mor* 3C 78
Coltness *N Lan* 4A 32
Col Uarach *W Isl* 3F 97
Colvend *Dum* 2D 7
Colvister *Shet* 2H 101
Comers *Abers* 1B 60
Comrie *Fife* 1C 32
Comrie *Per* 1C 40
Conaglen *High* 1B 46
Conchra *Arg* 1E 29
Conchra *High* 3B 64
Condorrat *N Lan* 2F 31
Conicaval *Mor* 4A 78
Conisby *Arg* 3C 26
Connel *Arg* 4A 46
Connel Park *E Ayr* 4B 20
Connista *High* 2D 73
Conon Bridge *High* 4C 76
Cononsyth *Ang* 3E 51
Conordan *High* 2E 63
Contin *High* 4B 76
Contullich *High* 2D 77
Cookney *Abers* 2D 61
Copister *Shet* 4G 101
Copshaw Holm *Bord* 3D 15
Cordon *N Ayr* 2B 18
Corgarff *Abers* 1D 59
Corlae *Dum* 2B 12
Cormiston *S Lan* 2F 21
Cornaigbeg *Arg* 3E 91
Cornaigmore *Arg* 1H 91
(nr Coll)
Cornaigmore *Arg* 3E 91
(nr Tiree)
Cornhill *Abers* 4A 80
Cornhill *High* 4A 84
Cornhill-on-Tweed *Nmbd* 2B 24
Cornquoy *Orkn* 2D 98
Corntown *High* 4C 76
Corpach *High* 4D 55
Corra *Dum* 1D 7
Corran *High* 1B 46
(nr Arnisdale)
Corran *High* 1B 54
(nr Fort William)
Corribeg *High* 4C 54
Corrie *N Ayr* 1B 18
Corrie Common *Dum* 3B 14
Corriecravie *N Ayr* 3A 18
Corriekinloch *High* 1E 83
Corriemoillie *High* 3A 76
Corrievarkie Lodge *Per* 4C 56
Corrievorrie *High* 3E 67
Corrigall *Orkn* 1B 98
Corrimony *High* 2A 66
Corrour Shooting Lodge
High 1F 47
Corry *High* 3F 63
Corrybrough *High* 3F 67
Corrygills *N Ayr* 2B 18
Corry of Ardnagrask *High* 1C 66
Corsback *High* 5A 98
(nr Dunnet)
Corsback *High* 2B 90
(nr Halkirk)
Corse *Abers* 1B 70
Corsehill *Abers* 4E 81
Corse of Kinnoir *Abers* 1A 70
Corsock *Dum* 4C 12
Corstorphine *Edin* 2E 33
Cortachy *Ang* 2C 50
Corwar House *S Ayr* 3D 11
Costa *Orkn* 5E 99
Cotehill *Cumb* 2D 9
Cothal *Abers* 4D 71
Cott *Orkn* 5H 99
Cottartown *High* 2B 68
Cottown *Abers* 1D 71
Coulags *High* 1C 64
Coulin Lodge *High* 4D 75
Coull *Abers* 1A 60
Coulport *Arg* 1A 30
Coulter *S Lan* 2F 21
Coupar Angus *Per* 3B 50
Coupland *Nmbd* 2C 24
Cour *Arg* 1F 17
Courance *Dum* 2F 13
Courteachan *High* 2F 53
Cousland *Midl* 3F 33
Coustonn *Arg* 2E 29
Cove *Arg* 1A 30
Cove *Bord* 2D 35
Cove *High* 1B 74
Cove Bay *Aber* 1E 61
Covesea *Mor* 2C 78
Covington *S Lan* 2E 21
Cowdenbeath *Fife* 4A 42
Cowdenburn *Bord* 4E 33
Cowdenend *Fife* 4A 42
Cowfords *Mor* 3E 79
Cowie *Abers* 3D 61
Cowie *Stir* 1A 32
Cowstrandburn *Fife* 4F 41
Coylton *S Ayr* 4F 19
Coylumbridge *High* 4A 68
Coynach *Abers* 1F 59
Coynachie *Abers* 2F 69
Crackaig *High* 2E 85
Cradhlastadh *W Isl* 3B 96
Cragabus *Arg* 1A 16
Craggan *High* 3B 68
Cragganmore *Mor* 2C 68
Cragganvallie *High* 2C 66
Craggie *High* 2D 85
Craggiemore *High* 2E 67
Craichie *Ang* 3E 51
Craig *High* 1D 65
(nr Achnashellach)
Craig *High* 3A 74
(nr Lower Diabaig)
Craig *High* 2B 64
(nr Stromeferry)
Craig *Arg* 4B 46
Craig *Dum* 4B 12
Craiganour Lodge *Per* 2B 48
Craigbrack *Arg* 4C 38
Craigdallie *Per* 1B 42
Craigdam *Abers* 2D 71
Craigdarroch *E Ayr* 1B 12
Craigdarroch *High* 4B 76
Craigdhu *High* 1B 66
Craigearn *Abers* 4C 70
Craigellachie *Mor* 1D 69
Craigend *Per* 1A 42
Craigendoran *Arg* 1B 30
Craigends *Ren* 3C 30
Craigenputtock *Dum* 3C 12
Craigens *E Ayr* 4A 20
Craighall *Edin* 2D 33
Craighead *Fife* 2F 43
Craighouse *Arg* 3F 27
Craigie *Per* 3A 50
(nr Blairgowrie)
Craigie *Per* 1A 42
(nr Perth)
Craigie *Abers* 4E 71
Craigie *D'dee* 4D 51
Craigie *S Ayr* 2F 19
Craigielaw *E Lot* 2A 34
Craiglemine *Dum* 4F 5
Craiglockhart *Edin* 2E 33
Craig Lodge *Arg* 2E 29
Craigmalloch *E Ayr* 2F 11
Craigmaud *Abers* 4D 81
Craigmill *Stir* 4D 41
Craigmillar *Edin* 2E 33
Craigmore *Arg* 3F 29
Craigmuie *Dum* 3C 12
Craignair *Dum* 1D 7
Craigneuk *N Lan* 3F 31
(nr Airdrie)
Craigneuk *N Lan* 4F 31
(nr Motherwell)
Craignure *Arg* 4E 45
Craigo *Ang* 1F 51
Craigrory *High* 1D 67
Craigrothie *Fife* 2C 42
Craigs *Dum* 4B 14
Craigs, The *High* 4F 83
Craigshill *W Lot* 3C 32
Craigton *Ang* 4E 51
(nr Carnoustie)
Craigton *Ang* 2C 50
(nr Kirriemuir)
Craigton *Aber* 1D 61
Craigton *Abers* 1C 60
Craigton *High* 1D 67
Craigtown *High* 2D 89
Craik *Bord* 1C 14
Crail *Fife* 3F 43
Crailing *Bord* 3F 23
Crailinghall *Bord* 3F 23
Cramond *Edin* 2D 33
Cramond Bridge *Edin* 2D 33
Cranloch *Mor* 4D 79
Crannich *Arg* 3C 44
Crannoch *Mor* 4F 79
Cranshaws *Bord* 3C 34
Craobh Haven *Arg* 3E 37
Craobhnaclag *High* 1B 66
Crarae *Arg* 4A 38
Crask *High* 1C 88
(nr Bettyhill)
Crask *High* 1A 84
(nr Lairg)
Crask of Aigas *High* 1B 66
Craster *Nmbd* 3F 25
Crathes *Abers* 2C 60
Crathie *Abers* 2D 59
Crathie *High* 2C 56
Crawford *S Lan* 3E 21
Crawforddyke *S Lan* 4A 32
Crawfordjohn *S Lan* 3D 21
Crawick *Dum* 4C 20
Crawton *Abers* 3D 61
Cray *Per* 1A 50
Creagan *Arg* 3A 46
Creag Aoil *High* 4E 55
Creag Ghoraidh *W Isl* 3G 93
Creaguaineach Lodge *High* 1E 47
Creca *Dum* 4B 14
Creebridge *Dum* 1F 5
Creetown *Dum* 2F 5
Creggans *Arg* 3B 38
Creich *Arg* 1A 36
Creich *Fife* 1C 42
Crepkill *High* 1D 63
Crianlarich *Stir* 1E 39
Crichton *Midl* 3F 33
Crieff *Per* 1D 41
Crimond *Abers* 4F 81
Crimonmogate *Abers* 4F 81
Crinan *Arg* 4E 37
Crocketford *Dum* 4D 13
Croftamie *Stir* 1C 30
Croftfoot *Glas* 3D 31
Croftmill *Per* 4D 49
Crofton *Cumb* 2C 8
Crofts *Dum* 4C 12
Crofts of Benachielt *High* 4A 90
Crofts of Dipple *Mor* 4E 79
Croggan *Arg* 1E 37
Croglin *Cumb* 3E 9
Croich *High* 4F 83
Croick *High* 2D 89
Croig *Arg* 2A 44
Cromarty *High* 3E 77
Crombie *Fife* 1C 32
Cromdale *High* 3B 68
Cromor *W Isl* 4F 97
Cromra *High* 3C 56
Cronberry *E Ayr* 3B 20
Crookdake *Cumb* 3A 8
Crookedholm *E Ayr* 2F 19
Crookham *Nmbd* 2C 24
Crook of Devon *Per* 3F 41
Crookston *Glas* 3D 31
Cros *W Isl* 1G 97
Crosbie *N Ayr* 4A 30
Crosbost *W Isl* 4E 97
Crosby *Cumb* 4F 7
Crosby Villa *Cumb* 4F 7
Crossaig *Arg* 4C 28
Crossapol *Arg* 3E 91
Crosscanonby *Cumb* 4F 7
Crossford *Fife* 1C 32
Crossford *S Lan* 1D 21
Crossgate *Orkn* 1C 98
Crossgatehall *E Lot* 3F 33
Crossgates *Fife* 1D 33
Crosshands *E Ayr* 2F 19
Crosshill *E Ayr* 3F 19
Crosshill *Fife* 4A 42
Crosshill *S Ayr* 1E 11
Crosshills *High* 2D 77
Crosshouse *E Ayr* 2E 19
Crossings *Cumb* 4E 15
Crosskirk *High* 1F 89
Crosslee *Ren* 3C 30
Crossmichael *Dum* 1C 6
Cross of Jackston *Abers* 2C 70
Crossroads *Abers* 1E 61
(nr Aberdeen)
Crossroads *Abers* 2C 60
(nr Banchory)
Crossroads *E Ayr* 2F 19
Crosston *Ang* 2E 51
Crothair *W Isl* 3C 96
Crovie *Abers* 3D 81
Croy *High* 1E 67
Croy *N Lan* 2F 31
Crubenbeg *High* 2D 57
Crubenmore Lodge *High* 2D 57
Cruden Bay *Abers* 2F 71
Crudie *Abers* 4C 80
Crulabhig *W Isl* 3C 96
Cuaich *High* 3D 57
Cuaig *High* 4A 74
Cuan *Arg* 2E 37
Cuckron *Shet* 1C 100
Cuidhir *W Isl* 2B 92
Cuidhsiadar *W Isl* 1G 97
Cuidhtinis *W Isl* 4E 95
Culbo *High* 3D 77
Culbokie *High* 4D 77
Culburnie *High* 1B 66
Culcabock *High* 1D 67
Culcharry *High* 4F 77
Culduie *High* 1A 64
Culeave *High* 4A 84
Culgaith *Cumb* 4F 9
Culkein *High* 4B 86
Culkein Drumbeg *High* 4C 86
Cullen *Mor* 3A 80
Cullicudden *High* 3D 77
Cullipool *Arg* 2E 37
Cullivoe *Shet* 1H 101
Culloch *Per* 2C 40
Culloden *High* 1E 67
Cul na Caepaich *High* 3F 53
Culnacnoc *High* 3E 73
Culnacraig *High* 3B 82
Culrain *High* 4A 84
Culross *Fife* 1B 32
Culroy *S Ayr* 4E 19
Culswick *Shet* 2A 100
Cults *Aber* 1D 61
Cults *Abers* 2A 70
Cults *Fife* 3C 42
Cultybraggan Camp *Per* 1C 40
Culzie Lodge *High* 2C 76
Cumbernauld *N Lan* 2F 31
Cumbernauld Village *N Lan* 2F 31
Cumdivock *Cumb* 3C 8
Cuminestown *Abers* 4D 81
Cumledge Mill *Bord* 4D 35
Cumlewick *Shet* 4C 100
Cummersdale *Cumb* 2C 8
Cummertrees *Dum* 1A 8
Cummingstown *Mor* 3C 78
Cumnock *E Ayr* 3A 20
Cumrew *Cumb* 2E 9
Cumwhinton *Cumb* 2D 9
Cumwhitton *Cumb* 2E 9
Cunninghamhead *N Ayr* 1E 19
Cunning Park *S Ayr* 4E 19
Cunningsburgh *Shet* 4C 100
Cunnister *Shet* 2H 101
Cupar *Fife* 2C 42
Cupar Muir *Fife* 2C 42
Currie *Edin* 3D 33
Cuthill *E Lot* 2F 33
Cutts *Shet* 3B 100
Cuttyhill *Abers* 4F 81

D

Dacre *Cumb* 4D 9
Dail *Arg* 4B 46
Dail Beag *W Isl* 2D 96
Dail bho Dheas *W Isl* 1F 97
Dailly *S Ayr* 1D 11
Dail Mor *W Isl* 2D 96
Dairsie *Fife* 2D 43
Dalabrog *W Isl* 5G 93
Dalavich *Arg* 2A 38
Dalbeattie *Dum* 1D 7
Dalblair *E Ayr* 4B 20
Dalchalm *High* 3E 85
Dalcharn *High* 2B 88
Dalchork *High* 2A 84
Dalchreichart *High* 4F 65
Dalchruin *Per* 2C 40
Dalcross *High* 1E 67
Dale *Cumb* 3E 9
Dalelia *High* 1E 45
Dale of Walls *Shet* 1A 100
Dalgarven *N Ayr* 1D 19
Dalgety Bay *Fife* 1D 33
Dalginross *Per* 1C 40
Dalguise *Per* 3E 49
Dalhalvaig *High* 2D 89
Dalintart *Arg* 1F 37
Dalkeith *Midl* 3F 33
Dallas *Mor* 4C 78
Dalleagles *E Ayr* 4A 20
Dall House *Per* 2A 48
Dalmally *Arg* 1C 38
Dalmarnock *Glas* 3E 31
Dalmellington *E Ayr* 1F 11
Dalmeny *Edin* 2D 33
Dalmigavie *High* 4E 67
Dalmilling *S Ayr* 3E 19
Dalmore *High* 3D 77
(nr Alness)
Dalmore *High* 3C 84
(nr Rogart)
Dalmuir *W Dun* 2C 30
Dalmunach *Mor* 1D 69
Dalnabreck *High* 1E 45
Dalnacardoch Lodge *Per* 4E 57
Dalnamein Lodge *Per* 1C 48
Dalnaspidal Lodge *Per* 4D 57
Dalnatrat *High* 2A 46
Dalnavie *High* 2D 77
Dalnawillan Lodge *High* 3F 89
Dalness *High* 2C 46
Dalnessie *High* 2B 84
Dalqueich *Per* 3F 41
Dalquhairn *S Ayr* 2E 11
Dalreavoch *High* 3C 84
Dalreoch *Per* 2F 41
Dalry *Edin* 2E 33
Dalry *N Ayr* 1D 19
Dalrymple *E Ayr* 4E 19
Dalserf *S Lan* 4A 32
Dalsmirren *Arg* 4D 17
Dalston *Cumb* 2C 8

Dalswinton – Flatt, The

Dalswinton *Dum* 3E **13**
Dalton *Dum* 4A **14**
Dalton *S Lan* 4E **31**
Daltot *Arg* 1B **28**
Dalvey *High* 2C **68**
Dalwhinnie *High* 3D **57**
Damhead *Mor* 4B **78**
Danderhall *Midl* 3F **33**
Danestone *Aber* 4E **71**
Dargill *Per* 2D **41**
Darnford *Abers* 2C **60**
Darnick *Bord* 2E **23**
Darra *Abers* 1C **70**
Dartfield *Abers* 4F **81**
Darvel *E Ayr* 2A **20**
Dava *Mor* 2B **68**
Davidson's Mains *Edin* 2E **33**
Davidston *High* 3E **77**
Davington *Dum* 1B **14**
Daviot *Abers* 3C **70**
Daviot *High* 2E **67**
Deadwater *Nmbd* 2F **15**
Dean *Cumb* 4F **7**
Deanburnhaugh *Bord* 4C **22**
Deanich Lodge *High* 1A **76**
Deans *W Lot* 3C **32**
Deanscales *Cumb* 4F **7**
Deanston *Stir* 3C **40**
Dearham *Cumb* 4F **7**
Dechmont *W Lot* 2C **32**
Deebank *Abers* 2B **60**
Deerhill *Mor* 4F **79**
Deerness *Orkn* 2D **98**
Delfour *High* 1F **57**
Delliefure *High* 2B **68**
Delny *High* 2E **77**
Den, The *N Ayr* 4B **30**
Denbeath *Fife* 4C **42**
Denhead *Abers* 2E **71**
(nr Ellon)
Denhead *Abers* 4E **81**
(nr Strichen)
Denhead *Fife* 2D **43**
Denholm *Bord* 4E **23**
Denny *Falk* 1A **32**
Dennyloanhead *Falk* 1A **32**
Den of Lindores *Fife* 2B **42**
Denside *Abers* 2D **61**
Denwick *Nmbd* 4F **25**
Derculich *Per* 2D **49**
Derryguaig *Arg* 4B **44**
Dervaig *Arg* 2B **44**
Detchant *Nmbd* 2D **25**
Deuchar *Ang* 1D **51**
Devonside *Clac* 4E **41**
Dewartown *Midl* 3F **33**
Digg *High* 3D **73**
Dillarburn *S Lan* 1D **21**
Dingleton *Bord* 2E **23**
Dingwall *High* 4C **76**
Dinnet *Abers* 2F **59**
Dippen *Arg* 2E **17**
Dippin *N Ayr* 3B **18**
Dipple *S Ayr* 1D **11**
Dirleton *E Lot* 1B **34**
Dishes *Orkn* 5H **99**
Distington *Cumb* 4F **7**
Divach *High* 3B **66**
Dixonfield *High* 1A **90**
Dochgarroch *High* 1D **67**
Doddington *Nmbd* 2C **24**
Doll *High* 3D **85**
Dollar *Clac* 4E **41**
Dolphinton *S Lan* 1A **22**
Doonfoot *S Ayr* 4E **19**
Doonholm *S Ayr* 4E **19**
Dorback Lodge *High* 4B **68**
Dores *High* 2C **66**
Dornie *High* 3B **64**
Dornoch *High* 1E **77**
Dornock *Dum* 1B **8**
Dorrery *High* 2F **89**
Dougarie *N Ayr* 2F **17**
Douglas *S Lan* 2D **21**
Douglastown *Ang* 3D **51**
Douglas Water *S Lan* 2D **21**
Dounby *Orkn* 1A **98**
Doune *High* 4F **67**
(nr Kingussie)
Doune *High* 3F **83**
(nr Lairg)
Doune *Stir* 3C **40**
Dounie *High* 4A **84**
(nr Bonar Bridge)
Dounie *High* 1D **77**
(nr Tain)
Dounreay, Upper & Lower *High* 1E **89**
Doura *N Ayr* 1E **19**
Dovenby *Cumb* 4F **7**
Dowally *Per* 3F **49**
Downfield *D'dee* 4C **50**
Downham *Nmbd* 2B **24**
Downies *Abers* 2E **61**
Doxford *Nmbd* 3E **25**
Draffan *S Lan* 1C **20**
Drakemyre *N Ayr* 4A **30**
Dreghorn *N Ayr* 2E **19**
Drem *E Lot* 2B **34**
Dreumasdal *W Isl* 4G **93**
Drimnin *High* 2C **44**
Drinisiadar *W Isl* 3F **95**
Droman *High* 2C **86**
Dron *Per* 2A **42**
Drongan *E Ayr* 4F **19**
Dronley *Ang* 4C **50**
Druim *High* 4A **78**
Druimarbin *High* 4D **55**
Druim Fhearna *High* 4F **63**
Druimindarroch *High* 3F **53**
Druim Saighdinis *W Isl* 1H **93**
Drum *Per* 3F **41**
Drumbeg *High* 4C **86**
Drumblade *Abers* 1A **70**
Drumbuie *Dum* 3A **12**
Drumbuie *High* 2A **64**
Drumburgh *Cumb* 2B **8**
Drumburn *Dum* 1E **7**
Drumchapel *Glas* 2D **31**
Drumchardine *High* 1C **66**
Drumchork *High* 1B **74**
Drumclog *S Lan* 2B **20**
Drumeldrie *Fife* 3D **43**
Drumelzier *Bord* 2A **22**
Drumfearn *High* 4F **63**
Drumgask *High* 2D **57**
Drumgelloch *N Lan* 3F **31**
Drumgley *Ang* 2D **51**
Drumguish *High* 2E **57**
Drumin *Mor* 2C **68**
Drumindorsair *High* 1B **66**
Drumlamford House *S Ayr* 4D **11**
Drumlasie *Abers* 1B **60**
Drumlemble *Arg* 4D **17**
Drumlithie *Abers* 3C **60**
Drummoddie *Dum* 3E **5**
Drummond *High* 3D **77**
Drummore *Dum* 4C **4**
Drummuir *Mor* 1E **69**
Drumnadrochit *High* 2C **66**
Drumnagorrach *Mor* 4A **80**
Drumoak *Abers* 2C **60**
Drumrunie *High* 3C **82**
Drumry *W Dun* 2D **31**
Drums *Abers* 3E **71**
Drumsleet *Dum* 4E **13**
Drumsmittal *High* 1D **67**
Drums of Park *Abers* 4A **80**
Drumsturdy *Ang* 4D **51**
Drumtochty Castle *Abers* 3B **60**
Drumuie *High* 1D **63**
Drumuillie *High* 3A **68**
Drumvaich *Stir* 3B **40**
Drumwhindle *Abers* 2E **71**
Drunkendub *Ang* 3F **51**
Drybridge *Mor* 3F **79**
Drybridge *N Ayr* 2E **19**
Dryburgh *Bord* 2E **23**
Drymen *Stir* 1C **30**
Drymuir *Abers* 1E **71**
Drynachan Lodge *High* 2F **67**
Drynie Park *High* 4C **76**
Drynoch *High* 2D **63**
Dubford *Abers* 3C **80**
Dubiton *Abers* 4B **80**
Dubton *Ang* 2E **51**
Duchally *High* 2E **83**
Duddingston *Edin* 2E **33**
Duddo *Nmbd* 1C **24**
Dufftown *Mor* 1E **69**
Duffus *Mor* 3C **78**
Dufton *Cumb* 4F **9**
Duirinish *High* 2A **64**
Duisdalemore *High* 4F **63**
Duisdeil Mòr *High* 4F **63**
Duisky *High* 4D **55**
Dull *Per* 3D **49**
Dullatur *N Lan* 2F **31**
Dulnain Bridge *High* 3A **68**
Dumbarton *W Dun* 2C **30**
Dumfin *Arg* 1B **30**
Dumfries *Dum* **103** (4E **13**)
Dumgoyne *Stir* 1D **31**
Dun *Ang* 1F **51**
Dunagoil *Arg* 4E **29**
Dunalastair *Per* 2C **48**
Dunan *High* 3E **63**
Dunbar *E Lot* 2C **34**
Dunbeath *High* 4A **90**
Dunbeg *Arg* 4F **45**
Dunblane *Stir* 3C **40**
Dunbog *Fife* 2B **42**
Duncanston *Abers* 3A **70**
Duncanston *High* 4C **76**
Dun Charlabhaigh *W Isl* 2C **96**
Duncow *Dum* 3E **13**
Duncrievie *Per* 3A **42**
Dundee *D'dee* **103** (4D **51**)
Dundee Airport *D'dee* 1C **42**
Dundonald *S Ayr* 2E **19**
Dundonnell *High* 1D **75**
Dundraw *Cumb* 3B **8**
Dundreggan *High* 4A **66**
Dundrennan *Dum* 3C **6**
Dunecht *Abers* 1C **60**
Dunfermline *Fife* **103** (1C **32**)
Dunino *Fife* 2E **43**
Dunipace *Falk* 1A **32**
Dunira *Per* 1C **40**
Dunkeld *Per* 3F **49**
Dunlappie *Ang* 1E **51**
Dunlichity Lodge *High* 2D **67**
Dunlop *E Ayr* 1F **19**
Dunmaglass Lodge *High* 3C **66**
Dunmore *Arg* 3B **28**
Dunmore *Falk* 1A **32**
Dunmore *High* 1C **66**
Dunnet *High* 5A **98**
Dunnichen *Ang* 3E **51**
Dunning *Per* 2F **41**
Dunoon *Arg* 2F **29**
Dunphail *Mor* 1B **68**
Dunragit *Dum* 2C **4**
Dunrostan *Arg* 1B **28**
Duns *Bord* 4D **35**
Dunscore *Dum* 3D **13**
Dunshalt *Fife* 2B **42**
Dunshillock *Abers* 1E **71**
Dunstan *Nmbd* 4F **25**
Dunsyre *S Lan* 1F **21**
Duntocher *W Dun* 2C **30**
Duntulm *High* 2D **73**
Dunure *S Ayr* 4D **19**
Dunvegan *High* 1B **62**
Durdar *Cumb* 2D **9**
Durisdeer *Dum* 1D **13**
Durisdeermill *Dum* 1D **13**
Durnamuck *High* 4B **82**
Durness *High* 1F **87**
Durno *Abers* 3C **70**
Duror *High* 2A **46**
Durran *Arg* 3A **38**
Durran *High* 1A **90**
Dury *Shet* 1C **100**
Duthil *High* 3A **68**
Dyce *Aber* 4D **71**
Dyke *Mor* 4A **78**
Dykehead *Ang* 1C **50**
Dykehead *N Lan* 3A **32**
Dykehead *Stir* 4A **40**
Dykend *Ang* 2B **50**
Dykesfield *Cumb* 2C **8**
Dysart *Fife* 4C **42**

E

Eadar Dha Fhadhail *W Isl* 3B **96**
Eaglesfield *Cumb* 4F **7**
Eaglesfield *Dum* 4B **14**
Eaglesham *E Ren* 4D **31**
Eallabus *Arg* 3D **27**
Eals *Nmbd* 2F **9**
Eamont Bridge *Cumb* 4E **9**
Earlais *High* 3C **72**
Earle *Nmbd* 3C **24**
Earlish *High* 3C **72**
Earlsferry *Fife* 3D **43**
Earlsford *Abers* 2D **71**
Earlston *Bord* 2E **23**
Earlston *E Ayr* 2F **19**
Earlstoun *Dum* 3B **12**
Earlyvale *Bord* 4E **33**
Earsairidh *W Isl* 3C **92**
Easdale *Arg* 2E **37**
Easington *Nmbd* 2E **25**
Eassie *Ang* 3C **50**
Eassie and Nevay *Ang* 3C **50**
East Barns *E Lot* 2D **35**
East Bennan *N Ayr* 3A **18**
East Bolton *Nmbd* 4E **25**
East Burrafirth *Shet* 1B **100**
East Calder *W Lot* 3C **32**
East Clyne *High* 3D **85**
East Clyth *High* 4B **90**
East Croachy *High* 3D **67**
Easter Ardross *High* 2D **77**
Easter Balgedie *Per* 3A **42**
Easter Balmoral *Abers* 2D **59**
Easter Brae *High* 3D **77**
Easter Buckieburn *Stir* 1F **31**
Easter Fearn *High* 1D **77**
Easter Galcantray *High* 1F **67**
Easterhouse *Glas* 3E **31**
Easter Howgate *Midl* 3E **33**
Easter Kinkell *High* 4C **76**
Easter Lednathie *Ang* 1C **50**
Easter Ogil *Ang* 1D **51**
Easter Ord *Abers* 1D **61**
Easter Quarff *Shet* 3C **100**
Easter Rhynd *Per* 2A **42**
Easter Skeld *Shet* 2B **100**
Easter Suddie *High* 4D **77**
Easter Tulloch *Abers* 4C **60**
Eastfield *N Lan* 3A **32**
(nr Caldercruix)
Eastfield *N Lan* 3A **32**
(nr Harthill)
Eastfield *S Lan* 3E **31**
Eastfield Hall *Nmbd* 4F **25**
East Fortune *E Lot* 2B **34**
East Haven *Ang* 4E **51**
East Helmsdale *High* 2F **85**
East Horton *Nmbd* 2D **25**
Easthouses *Midl* 3F **33**
East Kilbride *S Lan* 4E **31**
East Kyloe *Nmbd* 2D **25**
East Langwell *High* 3C **84**
East Learmouth *Nmbd* 2B **24**
East Lilburn *Nmbd* 3D **25**
East Linton *E Lot* 2B **34**
East Mains *Abers* 2B **60**
East Mey *High* 5B **98**
Easton *Cumb* 2B **8**
(nr Burgh by Sands)
Easton *Cumb* 4D **15**
(nr Longtown)
East Ord *Nmbd* 4F **35**
East Pitcorthie *Fife* 3E **43**
East Rhidorroch Lodge *High* 4D **83**
Eastriggs *Dum* 1B **8**
East Saltoun *E Lot* 3A **34**
Eastshore *Shet* 5B **100**
East Wemyss *Fife* 4C **42**
East Whitburn *W Lot* 3B **32**
Eastwick *Shet* 4F **101**
Ecclefechan *Dum* 4A **14**
Eccles *Bord* 1A **24**
Ecclesmachan *W Lot* 2C **32**
Echt *Abers* 1C **60**
Eckford *Bord* 3A **24**
Eday Airport *Orkn* 4G **99**
Edderside *Cumb* 3A **8**
Edderton *High* 1E **77**
Eddleston *Bord* 1B **22**
Eddlewood *S Lan* 4F **31**
Edendonich *Arg* 1C **38**
Edenhall *Cumb* 4E **9**
Edentaggart *Arg* 4E **39**
Edgehead *Midl* 3F **33**
Edinbane *High* 4C **72**
Edinburgh *Edin* **104** (2E **33**)
Edinburgh Airport *Edin* 2D **33**
Edlingham *Nmbd* 4E **25**
Edmonstone *Orkn* 5G **99**
Ednam *Bord* 2A **24**
Edrom *Bord* 4E **35**
Edzell *Ang* 1F **51**
Effirth *Shet* 1B **100**
Efstigarth *Shet* 2G **101**
Eglingham *Nmbd* 4E **25**
Eight Mile Burn *Midl* 4D **33**
Eignaig *High* 3E **45**
Eilanreach *High* 4B **64**
Eildon *Bord* 2E **23**
Eileanach Lodge *High* 3C **76**
Eilean Fhlodaigh *W Isl* 2H **93**
Eilean Iarmain *High* 4A **64**
Einacleit *W Isl* 4C **96**
Eisgein *W Isl* 1H **95**
Elcho *Per* 1A **42**
Elderslie *Ren* 3C **30**
Elford *Nmbd* 2E **25**
Elgin *Mor* 3D **79**
Elgol *High* 4E **63**
Elie *Fife* 3D **43**
Elizafield *Dum* 4F **13**
Ellan *High* 3F **67**
Ellary *Arg* 2B **28**
Ellemford *Bord* 3D **35**
Ellenabeich *Arg* 2E **37**
Ellenborough *Cumb* 4F **7**
Elleric *Arg* 3B **46**
Ellingham *Nmbd* 3E **25**
Elliot *Ang* 4F **51**
Ellishadder *High* 3E **73**
Ellon *Abers* 2E **71**
Ellonby *Cumb* 4D **9**
Elphin *High* 2D **83**
Elphinstone *E Lot* 2F **33**
Elrick *Abers* 1D **61**
Elrick *Mor* 3F **69**
Elrig *Dum* 3E **5**
Elsrickle *S Lan* 1F **21**
Elvanfoot *S Lan* 4E **21**
Elvingston *E Lot* 2A **34**
Elwick *Nmbd* 2E **25**
Embleton *Cumb* 4A **8**
Embleton *Nmbd* 3F **25**
Embo *High* 4D **85**
Embo Street *High* 4D **85**
Enoch *Dum* 1D **13**
Enochdhu *Per* 1F **49**
Ensay *Arg* 3A **44**
Enterkinfoot *Dum* 1D **13**
Eolaigearraidh *W Isl* 2C **92**
Eorabus *Arg* 1A **36**
Eoropaidh *W Isl* 1G **97**
Erbusaig *High* 3A **64**
Erchless Castle *High* 1B **66**
Eredine *Arg* 3A **38**
Eriboll *High* 2F **87**
Ericstane *Dum* 4F **21**
Erines *Arg* 2C **28**
Errogie *High* 3C **66**
Errol *Per* 1B **42**
Errol Station *Per* 1B **42**
Erskine *Ren* 2C **30**
Ervie *Dum* 1B **4**
Eskadale *High* 2B **66**
Eskbank *Midl* 3F **33**
Eskdalemuir *Dum* 2B **14**
Esknish *Arg* 3D **27**
Eslington Hall *Nmbd* 4D **25**
Essich *High* 2D **67**
Eswick *Shet* 1C **100**
Etal *Nmbd* 2C **24**
Ethie Haven *Ang* 3F **51**
Etteridge *High* 2D **57**
Ettrick *Bord* 4B **22**
Ettrickbridge *Bord* 3C **22**
Evanton *High* 3D **77**
Evelix *High* 4C **84**
Everbay *Orkn* 5H **99**
Evertown *Dum* 4C **14**
Ewes *Dum* 2C **14**
Exnaboe *Shet* 5B **100**
Eyemouth *Bord* 3F **35**
Eynort *High* 3C **62**
Eyre *High* 4D **73**
(nr Isle of Skye)
Eyre *High* 2E **63**
(nr Raasay)

F

Faichem *High* 1F **55**
Faifley *W Dun* 2D **31**
Fail *S Ayr* 3F **19**
Failford *S Ayr* 3F **19**
Fair Hill *Cumb* 4E **9**
Fairhill *S Lan* 4F **31**
Fair Isle Airport *Shet* 1H **99**
Fairlie *N Ayr* 4A **30**
Fairmilehead *Edin* 3E **33**
Fala *Midl* 3A **34**
Fala Dam *Midl* 3A **34**
Falkirk *Falk* **105** (1A **32**)
Falkland *Fife* 3B **42**
Fallin *Stir* 4D **41**
Falstone *Nmbd* 3F **15**
Fanagmore *High* 3C **86**
Fanellan *High* 1B **66**
Fankerton *Falk* 1F **31**
Fanmore *Arg* 3B **44**
Fannich Lodge *High* 3F **75**
Fans *Bord* 1F **23**
Farlam *Cumb* 2E **9**
Farley *High* 1B **66**
Farmtown *Mor* 4A **80**
Farnell *Ang* 2F **51**
Farr *High* 1C **88**
(nr Bettyhill)
Farr *High* 2D **67**
(nr Inverness)
Farr *High* 1F **57**
(nr Kingussie)
Farraline *High* 3C **66**
Fasag *High* 4B **74**
Fascadale *High* 4E **53**
Fasnacloich *Arg* 3B **46**
Fassfern *High* 4D **55**
Faugh *Cumb* 2E **9**
Fauldhouse *W Lot* 3B **32**
Feagour *High* 2C **56**
Fearann Dhomhnaill *High* 1F **53**
Fearn *High* 2F **77**
Fearnan *Per* 3C **48**
Fearnbeg *High* 4A **74**
Fearnmore *High* 3A **74**
Featherstone Castle *Nmbd* 1F **9**
Felkington *Nmbd* 1C **24**
Fell Side *Cumb* 4C **8**
Fenham *Nmbd* 1D **25**
Fenton *Cumb* 2E **9**
Fenton *Nmbd* 2C **24**
Fenton Barns *E Lot* 1B **34**
Fenwick *Nmbd* 1D **25**
Fenwick *E Ayr* 1F **19**
Feochaig *Arg* 4E **17**
Feolin Ferry *Arg* 3E **27**
Feorlan *Arg* 4D **17**
Ferindonald *High* 1F **53**
Feriniquarrie *High* 4A **72**
Fern *Ang* 1D **51**
Ferness *High* 1A **68**
Ferniefflatt *Abers* 4D **61**
Erniegair *S Lan* 4F **31**
Fernilea *High* 2C **62**
Ferryden *Ang* 2F **51**
Ferryhill *Aber* 1E **61**
Ferryton *High* 3D **77**
Fersit *High* 4A **56**
Feshiebridge *High* 1F **57**
Feshiebridge Airstrip *High* 1F **57**
Fetterangus *Abers* 4E **81**
Fettercairn *Abers* 4B **60**
Fiag Lodge *High* 1F **83**
Fidden *Arg* 1A **36**
Fieldhead *Cumb* 4D **9**
Fife Keith *Mor* 4F **79**
Finavon *Ang* 2D **51**
Fincharn *Arg* 3A **38**
Findhorn *Mor* 3B **78**
Findhorn Bridge *High* 3F **67**
Findochty *Mor* 3F **79**
Findo Gask *Per* 1F **41**
Findon *Abers* 2E **61**
Findon Mains *High* 3D **77**
Fingland *Cumb* 2B **8**
Fingland *Dum* 4C **20**
Finiskaig *High* 2B **54**
Finnart *Per* 2A **48**
Finnygaud *Abers* 4B **80**
Finstown *Orkn* 1B **98**
Fintry *Abers* 4C **80**
Fintry *D'dee* 4D **51**
Fintry *Stir* 1E **31**
Finzean *Abers* 2B **60**
Fionnphort *Arg* 1A **36**
Fionnsabhagh *W Isl* 4E **95**
First Coast *High* 4A **82**
Firth *Shet* 4G **101**
Fishcross *Clac* 4D **41**
Fisherford *Abers* 2B **70**
Fisherrow *E Lot* 2F **33**
Fisherton *High* 4E **77**
Fisherton *S Ayr* 4D **19**
Fishnish *Arg* 3D **45**
Fishwick *Bord* 4F **35**
Fiskavaig *High* 2C **62**
Fitch *Shet* 2B **100**
Fiunary *High* 3D **45**
Fladda *Shet* 3F **101**
Fladdabister *Shet* 3C **100**
Flashader *High* 4C **72**
Flatt, The *Cumb* 4E **15**

Fleck – Hazelbank

Fleck Shet 5B 100
Fleisirin W Isl 3G 97
Flemington S Lan 3E 31
(nr Glasgow)
Flemington S Lan 1C 20
(nr Strathaven)
Fleoideabhagh W Isl 4E 95
Fletchertown Cumb 3B 8
Fleuchary High 4C 84
Flimby Cumb 4F 7
Flodden Nmbd 2C 24
Flodigarry High 2D 73
Flushing Abers 1F 71
Fochabers Mor 4E 79
Fodderty High 4C 76
Foffarty Ang 3D 51
Fogo Bord 1A 24
Fogorig Bord 1A 24
Foindle High 3C 86
Folda Ang 1A 50
Folla Rule Abers 2C 70
Foodieash Fife 2C 42
Footdee Aber 1E 61
Forbestown Abers 4E 69
Ford Arg 3F 37
Ford Nmbd 2C 24
Fordell Fife 1D 33
Fordie Per 1C 40
Fordoun Abers 4C 60
Fordyce Abers 3A 80
Foresterseat Mor 4C 78
Forest Head Cumb 2E 9
Forest Lodge Per 4A 58
Forest Mill Clac 4E 41
Forfar Ang 2D 51
Forgandenny Per 2F 41
Forgewood N Lan 4F 31
Forgie Mor 4E 79
Forgue Abers 1B 70
Forneth Per 3F 49
Forres Mor 4B 78
Forrestfield N Lan 3A 32
Forrest Lodge Dum 3A 12
Forse High 4B 90
Forsinard High 3D 89
Forss High 1F 89
Fort Augustus High 1A 56
Forteviot Per 2F 41
Fort George High 4E 77
Forth S Lan 4B 32
Fortingall Per 3C 48
Fort Matilda Inv 2A 30
Fortrie Abers 1B 70
Fortrose High 4E 77
Fort William High 105 (4E 55)
Foss Per 2C 48
Fothergill Cumb 4F 7
Foubister Orkn 2D 98
Foula Airport Shet 4A 100
Foulbridge Cumb 3D 9
Foulden Bord 4F 35
Fountainhall Bord 1D 23
Foveran Abers 3E 71
Fowlershill Aber 4E 71
Fowlis Ang 4C 50
Fowlis Wester Per 1E 41
Foyers High 3B 66
Foynesfield High 4F 77
Fraserburgh Abers 3E 81
Freester Shet 1C 100
Frenich Stir 3F 39
Fresgoe High 1E 89
Freswick High 1C 90
Freuchie Fife 3B 42
Friockheim Ang 3E 51
Frobost W Isl 5G 93
Frotoft Orkn 5F 99
Fullwood E Ayr 4C 30
Funzie Shet 2H 101
Furnace Arg 3B 38
Fyvie Abers 2C 70

G

Gabhsann bho Dheas W Isl 1F 97
Gabhsann bho Thuath W Isl 1F 97
Gabroc Hill E Ayr 4C 30
Gadgirth S Ayr 3F 19
Gaick Lodge High 3E 57
Gairletter Arg 1F 29
Gairloch Abers 1C 60
Gairloch High 2B 74
Gairlochy High 3E 55
Gairney Bank Per 4A 42
Gairnshiel Lodge Abers 1D 59
Gaitsgill Cumb 3C 8
Galashiels Bord 2D 23
Gallatown Fife 4B 42
Gallin Per 3A 48
Gallowfauld Ang 3D 51
Gallowhill Per 4A 50
Gallowhill Ren 3C 30
Gallowhills Abers 4F 81
Galltair High 3B 64
Galmisdale High 3D 53
Galston E Ayr 2F 19
Galtrigill High 4A 72
Gamblesby Cumb 4F 9
Gamelsby Cumb 2B 8
Ganavan Arg 4F 45
Gannochy Ang 4A 60
Gannochy Per 1A 42
Gansclet High 3C 90
Garafad High 3D 73
Gardenstown Abers 3D 81
Garderhouse Shet 2B 100
Gardie Shet 1H 101
Gardie Ho Shet 2C 100
Garelochhead Arg 4D 39
Gargunnock Stir 4C 40
Garleffin S Ayr 3B 10
Garlieston Dum 3F 5
Garlogie Abers 1C 60
Garmond Abers 4D 81
Garmony Arg 3D 45
Garmouth Mor 3E 79
Garnkirk N Lan 3E 31
Garrabost W Isl 3G 97
Garrallan E Ayr 4A 20
Garrigill Cumb 3F 9
Garrogie Lodge High 4C 66
Garros High 3D 73
Garrow Per 3D 49
Gartcosh N Lan 3E 31
Garth Shet 1A 100
(nr Sandness)
Garth Shet 1C 100
(nr Skellister)
Garthamlock Glas 3E 31
Gartly Abers 2A 70
Gartmore Stir 4A 40
Gartness N Lan 3F 31
Gartness Stir 1D 31
Gartocharn W Dun 1C 30
Gartsherrie N Lan 3F 31
Gartymore High 2F 85
Garvald E Lot 2B 34
Garvamore High 2C 56
Garvard Arg 4A 36
Garvault High 4C 88
Garve High 3A 76
Garvie Arg 4B 38
Garvock Abers 4C 60
Garvock Inv 2A 30
Gaskan High 4B 54
Gatehead E Ayr 2E 19
Gatehouse of Fleet Dum 2B 6
Gatelawbridge Dum 2E 13
Gateside Ang 3D 51
(nr Forfar)
Gateside Ang 3C 50
(nr Kirriemuir)
Gateside Fife 3A 42
Gateside N Ayr 4B 30
Gattonside Bord 2E 23
Gauldry Fife 1C 42
Gavinton Bord 4D 35
Gayfield Orkn 2F 99
Geanies High 2F 77
Gearraidh Bhailteas W Isl 5G 93
Gearraidh Bhaird W Isl 1H 95
Gearraidh ma Monadh W Isl 1C 92
Gearraidh na h-Aibhne W Isl 3D 96
Geary High 3B 72
Geddes High 4F 77
Gedintailor High 2E 63
Geilston Arg 2B 30
Geirinis W Isl 3G 93
Geise High 1A 90
Geisiadar W Isl 3C 96
Gelder Shiel Abers 3D 59
Gellyburn Per 4F 49
Gelston Dum 2C 6
Geocrab W Isl 3F 95
Georgetown Ren 3C 30
Georth Orkn 5E 99
Gerston High 2A 90
Giffnock E Ren 4D 31
Gifford E Lot 3B 34
Giffordtown Fife 2B 42
Gilchriston E Lot 3A 34
Gilcrux Cumb 4A 8
Gillen High 4B 72
Gillock High 2B 90
Gills High 5B 98
Gilmanscleuch Bord 3C 22
Gilmerton Edin 3E 33
Gilmerton Per 1D 41
Gilsland Nmbd 1F 9
Gilsland Spa Cumb 1F 9
Gilston Bord 4A 34
Giosla W Isl 4C 96
Girdle Toll N Ayr 1E 19
Girlsta Shet 1C 100
Girthon Dum 2B 6
Girvan S Ayr 2C 10
Gladsmuir E Lot 2A 34
Glaichbea High 2C 66
Glame High 1E 63
Glamis Ang 3C 50
Glanton Nmbd 4D 25
Glanton Pyke Nmbd 4D 25
Glas Aird Arg 4A 36
Glas-allt Shiel Abers 3D 59
Glaschoil High 2B 68
Glasgow Glas 104 (3D 31)
Glasgow Airport Ren 3C 30
Glasgow Prestwick Airport S Ayr 3E 19
Glashvin High 3D 73
Glas na Cardaich High 2F 53
Glasnacardoch High 2F 53
Glasnakille High 4E 63
Glassburn High 2A 66
Glasserton Dum 4F 5
Glassford S Lan 1C 20
Glassgreen Mor 3D 79
Glasson Cumb 1B 8
Glassonby Cumb 4E 9
Glasterlaw Ang 2E 51
Gleann Dail bho Dheas W Isl 1C 92
Gleann Tholastaidh W Isl 2G 97
Gleann Uige High 4F 53
Glecknabae Arg 3E 29
Glen Dum 2A 6
Glenancross High 2F 53
Glenbarr Arg 2D 17
Glenbeg High 1C 44
Glen Bernisdale High 1D 63
Glenbervie Abers 3C 60
Glenboig N Lan 3F 31
Glenborrodale High 1D 45
Glenbranter Arg 4C 38
Glenbreck Bord 3F 21
Glenbrein Lodge High 4B 66
Glenbrittle High 3D 63
Glenbuchat Lodge Abers 4E 69
Glenbuck E Ayr 3C 20
Glenburn Ren 3C 30
Glencalvie Lodge High 1B 76
Glencaple Dum 1E 7
Glencarron Lodge High 4D 75
Glencarse Per 1A 42
Glencassley Castle High 3F 83
Glencat Abers 2A 60
Glencoe High 2C 46
Glen Cottage High 3F 53
Glencraig Fife 4A 42
Glendale High 1A 62
Glendevon Per 3E 41
Glendoebeg High 1B 56
Glendoick Per 1B 42
Glendoune S Ayr 2C 10
Glenduckie Fife 2B 42
Gleneagles Per 3E 41
Glenegedale Arg 4D 27
Glenegedale Lots Arg 4D 27
Glenelg High 4B 64
Glenernie Mor 1B 68
Glenesslin Dum 3D 13
Glenfarg Per 2A 42
Glenfarquhar Lodge Abers 3C 60
Glenferness Mains High 1A 68
Glenfeshie Lodge High 2F 57
Glenfiddich Lodge Mor 2E 69
Glenfinnan High 3C 54
Glenfintaig Lodge High 3F 55
Glenfoot Per 2A 42
Glenfyne Lodge Arg 2D 39
Glengap Dum 2B 6
Glengarnock N Ayr 4B 30
Glengolly High 1A 90
Glengorm Castle Arg 2B 44
Glengrasco High 1D 63
Glenhead Farm Ang 1B 50
Glenholm Bord 2A 22
Glen House Bord 2B 22
Glenhurich High 1F 45
Glenkerry Bord 4B 22
Glenkiln Dum 4D 13
Glenkindie Abers 4F 69
Glenkinglass Lodge Arg 4C 46
Glenkirk Bord 3F 21
Glenlean Arg 1E 29
Glenlee Dum 3B 12
Glenleraig High 4C 86
Glenlichorn Per 2C 40
Glenlivet Mor 3C 68
Glenlochar Dum 1C 6
Glenlochsie Lodge Per 4B 58
Glenluce Dum 2C 4
Glenmarksie High 4A 76
Glenmassan Arg 1F 29
Glenmavis N Lan 3F 31
Glenmazeran Lodge High 3E 67
Glenmidge Dum 3D 13
Glenmore High 1C 44
(nr Glenborrodale)
Glenmore High 1D 63
(nr Isle of Skye)
Glenmore High 1A 58
(nr Kingussie)
Glenmoy Ang 1D 51
Glennoe Arg 4B 46
Glen of Coachford Abers 1F 69
Glenogil Ang 1D 51
Glenprosen Village Ang 1C 50
Glenree N Ayr 3A 18
Glenrosa N Ayr 2B 18
Glenrothes Fife 3B 42
Glensanda High 3F 45
Glensaugh Abers 4B 60
Glenshero Lodge High 2C 56
Glensluain Arg 4B 38
Glenstockadale Dum 1B 4
Glenstriven Arg 2E 29
Glen Tanar House Abers 2F 59
Glenton Abers 3B 70
Glentress Bord 2B 22
Glentromie Lodge High 2E 57
Glentrool Lodge Dum 3F 11
Glentrool Village Dum 4E 11
Glentruim House High 2D 57
Glenuig High 4F 53
Glen Village Falk 2A 32
Glenwhilly Dum 4C 10
Glenzierfoot Dum 4C 14
Glespin S Lan 3D 21
Gletness Shet 1C 100
Glib Cheois W Isl 4E 97
Gloster Hill Nmbd 4F 25
Gloup Shet 1H 101
Glutt Lodge High 3E 89
Gobernuisgach Lodge High 3F 87
Gobernuisgeach High 4E 89
Gobhaig W Isl 2E 95
Gogar Edin 2D 33
Gollanfield High 4F 77
Golspie High 4D 85
Gometra House Arg 3A 44
Gonfirth Shet 5F 101
Gord Shet 4C 100
Gordon Bord 1F 23
Gordonbush High 3D 85
Gordonstown Abers 4A 80
(nr Cornhill)
Gordonstown Abers 2C 70
(nr Fyvie)
Gorebridge Midl 3F 33
Gorgie Edin 2E 33
Gorseness Orkn 1C 98
Gorstan High 3A 76
Gortantaoid Arg 2D 27
Gorteneorn High 1D 45
Gortenfern High 1D 45
Gossabrough Shet 3H 101
Goswick Nmbd 1D 25
Gott Arg 3F 91
Gott Shet 2C 100
Gourdon Abers 4D 61
Gourock Inv 2A 30
Govan Glas 3D 31
Govanhill Glas 3D 31
Gowanhill Abers 3F 81
Gowkhall Fife 1C 32
Grabhair W Isl 1H 95
Gramasdail W Isl 2H 93
Grandtully Per 2E 49
Grange E Ayr 2F 19
Grange Per 1B 42
Grange Crossroads Mor 4F 79
Grangemouth Falk 1B 32
Grange of Lindores Fife 2B 42
Grangepans Falk 1C 32
Granish High 4F 67
Grantlodge Abers 4C 70
Granton Edin 2E 33
Grantown-on-Spey High 3B 68
Grantshouse Bord 3E 35
Grassgarth Cumb 3C 8
Graven Shet 4G 101
Grayson Green Cumb 4E 7
Grealin High 3E 73
Great Blencow Cumb 4D 9
Great Broughton Cumb 4F 7
Great Clifton Cumb 4F 7
Great Corby Cumb 2D 9
Great Orton Cumb 2C 8
Great Ryle Nmbd 4D 25
Great Salkeld Cumb 4E 9
Greenbank Shet 1H 101
Greenburn W Lot 3B 32
Greendykes Nmbd 3D 25
Greenfield Arg 4D 39
Greenfoot N Lan 3F 31
Greengairs N Lan 2F 31
Greengill Cumb 4A 8
Greenhead Nmbd 1F 9
Greenhill Dum 4A 14
Greenhill Falk 2A 32
Greenhills N Ayr 4B 30
Greenholm E Ayr 2A 20
Greenigoe Orkn 2C 98
Greenland High 1B 90
Greenland Mains High 1B 90
Greenlaw Bord 1A 24
Greenlea Dum 4F 13
Greenloaning Per 3D 41
Greenmow Shet 4C 100
Greenock Inv 2A 30
Greenock Mains E Ayr 3B 20
Greenrow Cumb 2A 8
Greens Abers 1D 71
Greensidehill Nmbd 4C 24
Greenwall Orkn 2D 98
Greenwell Cumb 2E 9
Grein W Isl 2B 92
Greinetobht W Isl 5C 94
Gremista Shet 2C 100
Greosabhagh W Isl 3F 95
Greshornish High 4C 72
Gretna Dum 1C 8
Gretna Green Dum 1C 8
Greysouthen Cumb 4F 7
Greystoke Cumb 4D 9
Greystoke Gill Cumb 4D 9
Greystone Ang 3E 51
Griais W Isl 2F 97
Grianan W Isl 3F 97
Gribun Arg 4B 44
Grimbister Orkn 1B 98
Grimeston Orkn 1B 98
Griminis W Isl 2G 93
(nr Benbecula)
Griminis W Isl 5B 94
(nr North Uist)
Grimister Shet 2G 101
Grimness Orkn 3C 98
Grindiscol Shet 3C 100
Grindon Nmbd 1C 24
Grinsdale Cumb 2C 8
Griomsidar W Isl 4F 97
Grishipoll Arg 2G 91
Gritley Orkn 2D 98
Grobister Orkn 5H 99
Grobsness Shet 5F 101
Grogport Arg 1F 17
Groigearraidh W Isl 3G 93
Grove, The Dum 4E 13
Grudie High 3A 76
Gruids High 3A 84
Gruinard House High 4A 82
Gruinart Arg 3C 26
Grulinbeg Arg 3C 26
Gruline Arg 3C 44
Grummore High 4B 88
Gruting Shet 2A 100
Grutness Shet 5C 100
Gualachulain High 3C 46
Gualin House High 2E 87
Guardbridge Fife 2D 43
Guay Per 3F 49
Guildtown Per 4A 50
Gulberwick Shet 3C 100
Gullane E Lot 1A 34
Gunnista Shet 2C 100
Gunsgreenhill Bord 3F 35
Gutcher Shet 2H 101
Guthrie Ang 2E 51
Guyzance Nmbd 4F 25

H

Haa of Houlland Shet 1H 101
Hackland Orkn 5E 99
Hackness Orkn 3B 98
Haclait W Isl 3H 93
Hadden Bord 2A 24
Haddington E Lot 2B 34
Haddo Abers 2D 71
Haggbeck Cumb 4D 15
Haggersta Shet 2B 100
Haggerston Nmbd 1D 25
Haggrister Shet 4F 101
Halbeath Fife 1D 33
Halcro High 1B 90
Halistra High 4B 72
Halket E Ayr 4C 30
Halkirk High 2A 90
Hall E Ren 4C 30
Hallbankgate Cumb 2E 9
Halliburton Bord 1F 23
Hallin High 4B 72
Hallyne Bord 1A 22
Haltcliff Bridge Cumb 4C 8
Halton Lea Gate Nmbd 2F 9
Haltwhistle Nmbd 1F 9
Ham High 5A 98
Ham Shet 4A 100
Hamilton S Lan 105 (4F 31)
Hamister Shet 5H 101
Hamnavoe Shet 3E 101
(nr Braehoulland)
Hamnavoe Shet 3B 100
(nr Burland)
Hamnavoe Shet 4G 101
(nr Lunna)
Hamnavoe Shet 3G 101
(nr Yell)
Happas Ang 3D 51
Happendon S Lan 2D 21
Harbottle Nmbd 4C 24
Hardgate Abers 1C 60
Hardgate Dum 1D 7
Harehope Nmbd 3D 25
Harelaw Dum 4D 15
Haresceugh Cumb 3F 9
Hareshaw N Lan 3A 32
Harker Cumb 1C 8
Harkland Shet 3G 101
Harlosh High 1B 62
Haroldswick Shet 1H 101
Harpsdale High 2A 90
Harraby Cumb 2D 9
Harrapool High 3F 63
Harrapul High 3F 63
Harrietfield Per 1E 41
Harrington Cumb 4E 7
Harriston Cumb 3A 8
Harthill N Lan 3B 32
Hartmount Holdings High 2E 77
Hartwood N Lan 4A 32
Hassendean Bord 3E 23
Haster High 2C 90
Hastigrow High 1B 90
Hatton Abers 2F 71
Hattoncrook Abers 3D 71
Hatton of Fintray Abers 4D 71
Haugh E Ayr 3F 19
Haugh Head Nmbd 3D 25
Haugh of Ballechin Per 2E 49
Haugh of Glass Mor 2F 69
Haugh of Urr Dum 1D 7
Haunn Arg 3A 44
Haunn W Isl 1C 92
Hawick Bord 4E 23
Hawksdale Cumb 3C 8
Hayhill E Ayr 4F 19
Hayshead Ang 3F 51
Hayton Cumb 3A 8
(nr Aspatria)
Hayton Cumb 2E 9
(nr Brampton)
Hayton Aber 1E 61
Haywood S Lan 4B 32
Hazelbank S Lan 1D 21

Hazelton Walls – Kinloch Hourn

Hazelton Walls *Fife* 1C **42**
Hazon *Nmbd* 4E **25**
Head of Muir *Falk* 1A **32**
Heads Nook *Cumb* 2D **9**
Heanish *Arg* 3F **91**
Heaste *High* 4F **63**
Heatherfield *High* 1D **63**
Heathfield *Cumb* 3A **8**
Heathfield *Ren* 3B **30**
Heathhall *Dum* 4E **13**
Heck *Dum* 3F **13**
Heddle *Orkn* 1B **98**
Heglibister *Shet* 1B **100**
Heights of Brae *High* 3C **76**
Heights of Fodderty *High* 3C **76**
Heights of Kinlochewe *High* 3D **75**
Heiton *Bord* 2A **24**
Helensburgh *Arg* 1A **30**
Hellister *Shet* 2B **100**
Helmsdale *High* 2F **85**
Hempriggs *High* 3C **90**
Heogan *Shet* 2C **100**
Hepburn *Nmbd* 3D **25**
Heribusta *High* 2D **73**
Heriot *Bord* 4A **34**
Hermiston *Edin* 2D **33**
Hermitage *Bord* 2E **15**
Heronsford *S Ayr* 3C **10**
Herra *Shet* 2H **101**
Herston *Orkn* 3C **98**
Hesket Newmarket *Cumb* 4C **8**
Hessilhead *N Ayr* 4B **30**
Hestaford *Shet* 1A **100**
Hestinsetter *Shet* 2A **100**
Hestwall *Orkn* 1A **98**
Hethersgill *Cumb* 1D **9**
Hetherside *Cumb* 1D **9**
Hethpool *Nmbd* 3B **24**
Hetton Steads *Nmbd* 2D **25**
Heugh-head *Abers* 4E **69**
Heylipol *Arg* 3E **91**
High Auldgirth *Dum* 3E **13**
High Bankhill *Cumb* 3E **9**
High Banton *N Lan* 1F **31**
High Blantyre *S Lan* 4E **31**
High Bonnybridge *Falk* 2A **32**
Highbridge *Cumb* 3C **8**
Highbridge *High* 3F **55**
High Buston *Nmbd* 4F **25**
High Crosby *Cumb* 2D **9**
Highfield *N Ayr* 4B **30**
High Gallowhill *E Dun* 2E **31**
Highgate *N Ayr* 4B **30**
High Harrington *Cumb* 4F **7**
High Hesket *Cumb* 3D **9**
High Ireby *Cumb* 4B **8**
High Keil *Arg* 4D **17**
Highlaws *Cumb* 3A **8**
High Longthwaite *Cumb* 3B **8**
High Lorton *Cumb* 4A **8**
Highmoor *Cumb* 3B **8**
High Newton-by-the-Sea *Nmbd* 3F **25**
High Row *Cumb* 4C **8**
High Scales *Cumb* 3A **8**
High Side *Cumb* 4B **8**
Hightae *Dum* 4F **13**
High Trewhitt *Nmbd* 4D **25**
High Valleyfield *Fife* 1C **32**
Hillbrae *Abers* 1B **70** (nr Aberchirder)
Hillbrae *Abers* 3C **70** (nr Inverurie)
Hillbrae *Abers* 2D **71** (nr Methlick)
Hill End *Fife* 4F **41**
Hillend *Fife* 1D **33**
Hillend *N Lan* 3A **32**
Hillhead *Abers* 2A **70**
Hillhead *S Ayr* 4F **19**
Hillhead of Auchentumb *Abers* 4E **81**
Hilliclay *High* 1A **90**
Hillington *Glas* 3D **31**
Hill of Beath *Fife* 4A **42**
Hill of Fearn *High* 2F **77**
Hill of Fiddes *Abers* 3E **71**
Hill of Keillor *Ang* 3B **50**
Hill of Overbrae *Abers* 3D **81**
Hillside *Abers* 2E **61**
Hillside *Ang* 1F **51**
Hillside *Orkn* 5E **99**
Hillside *Shet* 5G **101**
Hillside of Prieston *Ang* 4C **50**
Hillswick *Shet* 4E **101**
Hillwell *Shet* 5B **100**
Hillyland *Per* 1F **41**
Hilton *High* 1E **77**
Hilton of Cadboll *High* 2F **77**
Hipsburn *Nmbd* 4F **25**
Hirn *Abers* 1C **60**
Hirst *N Lan* 3A **32**
Hobbister *Orkn* 2B **98**
Hobkirk *Bord* 4E **23**
Hoddomcross *Dum* 4A **14**
Hogaland *Shet* 4F **101**
Hogha Gearraidh *W Isl* 5B **94**
Holburn *Nmbd* 2D **25**
Holland *Orkn* 2F **99** (nr Papa Westray)
Holland *Orkn* 5H **99** (nr Stronsay)
Hollandstoun *Orkn* 2H **99**
Hollows *Dum* 4C **14**
Hollybush *E Ayr* 4E **19**
Holmend *Dum* 1F **13**
Holme St Cuthbert *Cumb* 3A **8**
Holmhead *E Ayr* 3A **20**
Holmisdale *High* 1A **62**
Holm of Drumlanrig *Dum* 2D **13**
Holmsgarth *Shet* 2C **100**
Holmwrangle *Cumb* 3E **9**
Holy Island *Nmbd* 1E **25**
Holytown *N Lan* 3F **31**
Holywood *Dum* 3E **13**
Hoove *Shet* 2B **100**
Hope *High* 1F **87**
Hopeman *Mor* 3C **78**
Horgabost *W Isl* 3E **95**
Horncliffe *Nmbd* 1C **24**
Horndean *Bord* 1B **24**
Hornsby *Cumb* 2E **9**
Hornsby Gate *Cumb* 2E **9**
Horsbrugh Ford *Bord* 2B **22**
Horsleyhill *Bord* 4E **23**
Hosh *Per* 1D **41**
Hosta *W Isl* 5B **94**
Hoswick *Shet* 4C **100**
Houbie *Shet* 2H **101**
Hough *Arg* 3E **91**
Houghton *Cumb* 2D **9**
Houlland *Shet* 1B **100** (nr Mainland)
Houlland *Shet* 4H **101** (nr Yell)
Houndslow *Bord* 1F **23**
Houndwood *Bord* 3E **35**
Housabister *Shet* 1C **100**
Househill *High* 4F **77**
Housetter *Shet* 3F **101**
Houss *Shet* 3B **100**
Houston *Ren* 3C **30**
Housty *High* 4A **90**
Houton *Orkn* 2B **98**
How *Cumb* 2E **9**
Howe *High* 1C **90**
Howe of Teuchar *Abers* 1C **70**
Howes *Dum* 1A **8**
Howgate *Midl* 4E **33**
Howick *Nmbd* 4F **25**
Hownam *Bord* 4A **24**
Howtel *Nmbd* 2B **24**
Howwood *Ren* 3B **30**
Hughton *High* 1B **66**
Huisinis *W Isl* 1D **94**
Humbie *E Lot* 3A **34**
Humbleton *Nmbd* 3C **24**
Hume *Bord* 1A **24**
Huna *High* 5B **98**
Hungladder *High* 2C **72**
Hunsonby *Cumb* 4E **9**
Hunspow *High* 5A **98**
Hunterfield *Midl* 3F **33**
Hunter's Quay *Arg* 2F **29**
Hunthill Lodge *Ang* 4F **59**
Huntington *E Lot* 2A **34**
Huntingtower *Per* 1F **41**
Huntly *Abers* 2A **70**
Huntlywood *Bord* 1F **23**
Hurlet *Glas* 3D **31**
Hurlford *E Ayr* 2F **19**
Hurliness *Orkn* 4A **98**
Hutton *Bord* 4F **35**
Hutton *Cumb* 4D **9**
Hutton End *Cumb* 4D **9**
Hutton Roof *Cumb* 4C **8**
Huxter *Shet* 1A **100** (nr Mainland)
Huxter *Shet* 5H **101** (nr Whalsay)
Hyndford Bridge *S Lan* 1E **21**
Hynish *Arg* 4E **91**
Hythie *Abers* 4F **81**

I

Ianstown *Mor* 3F **79**
Iarsiadar *W Isl* 3C **96**
Ibrox *Glas* 3D **31**
Ichrachan *Arg* 4B **46**
Idrigill *High* 3C **72**
Ilderton *Nmbd* 3D **25**
Imachar *N Ayr* 1F **17**
Inchbae Lodge *High* 3B **76**
Inchbare *Ang* 1F **51**
Inchberry *Mor* 4E **79**
Inchbraoch *Ang* 2F **51**
Incheril *High* 3D **75**
Inchinnan *Ren* 3C **30**
Inchlaggan *High* 1E **55**
Inchmichael *Per* 1B **42**
Inchnadamph *High* 1D **83**
Inchree *High* 1B **46**
Inchture *Per* 1B **42**
Inchyra *Per* 1A **42**
Ingram *Nmbd* 4D **25**
Inkstack *High* 5A **98**
Innellan *Arg* 3F **29**
Innerleith *Fife* 2B **42**
Innerleithen *Bord* 2C **22**
Innerleven *Fife* 3C **42**
Innermessan *Dum* 1B **4**
Innerwick *E Lot* 2D **35**
Innerwick *Per* 3A **48**
Insch *Abers* 3B **70**
Insh *High* 1F **57**
Inshegra *High* 2D **87**
Inshore *High* 1E **87**
Inver *Abers* 2D **59**
Inver *High* 1F **77**
Inver *Per* 3F **49**
Inverailort *High* 3A **54**
Inveralligin *High* 4B **74**
Inverallochy *Abers* 3F **81**
Inveramsay *Abers* 3C **70**
Inveran *High* 4A **84**
Inveraray *Arg* 3B **38**
Inverarish *High* 2E **63**
Inverarity *Ang* 3D **51**
Inverarnan *Stir* 2E **39**
Inverarnie *High* 2D **67**
Inverbeg *Arg* 4E **39**
Inverbervie *Abers* 4D **61**
Inverboyndie *Abers* 3B **80**
Invercassley *High* 3F **83**
Invercharnan *High* 3C **46**
Inverchoran *High* 4F **75**
Invercreran *Arg* 3B **46**
Inverdruie *High* 4A **68**
Inverebrie *Abers* 2E **71**
Invereck *Arg* 1F **29**
Inveresk *E Lot* 2F **33**
Inveresragan *Arg* 4A **46**
Inverey *Abers* 3B **58**
Inverfarigaig *High* 3C **66**
Invergarry *High* 1A **56**
Invergeldie *Per* 1C **40**
Invergordon *High* 3E **77**
Invergowrie *Per* 4C **50**
Inverguseran *High* 1A **54**
Inverharroch *Mor* 2E **69**
Inverie *High* 1A **54**
Inverinan *Arg* 2A **38**
Inverinate *High* 3C **64**
Inverkeilor *Ang* 3F **51**
Inverkeithing *Fife* 1D **33**
Inverkeithny *Abers* 1B **70**
Inverkip *Inv* 2A **30**
Inverkirkaig *High* 2B **82**
Inverlael *High* 1E **75**
Inverliever Lodge *Arg* 3F **37**
Inverliver *Arg* 4B **46**
Inverlochlarig *Stir* 2F **39**
Inverlochy *High* 4E **55**
Inverlussa *Arg* 1A **28**
Inver Mallie *High* 3E **55**
Invermarkie *Abers* 2F **69**
Invermoriston *High* 4B **66**
Invernaver *High* 1C **88**
Inverneil House *Arg* 1C **28**
Inverness *High* **105** (1D **67**)
Inverness Airport *High* 4E **77**
Invernettie *Abers* 1F **71**
Inverpolly Lodge *High* 2B **82**
Inverquhomery *Abers* 1F **71**
Inverroy *High* 3F **55**
Inversanda *High* 2A **46**
Invershiel *High* 4C **64**
Invershin *High* 4A **84**
Invershore *High* 4B **90**
Inversnaid *Stir* 3E **39**
Inverugie *Abers* 1F **71**
Inveruglas *Arg* 3E **39**
Inverurie *Abers* 3C **70**
Invervar *Per* 3B **48**
Inverythan *Abers* 1C **70**
Iochdar *W Isl* 3G **93**
Ireby *Cumb* 4B **8**
Ireland *Shet* 4B **100**
Irthington *Cumb* 1D **9**
Irvine *N Ayr* 2E **19**
Irvine Mains *N Ayr* 2E **19**
Isauld *High* 1E **89**
Isbister *Shet* 2F **101** (nr Mainland)
Isbister *Shet* 5H **101** (nr Whalsay)
Isbister *Orkn* 1B **98**
Islay Airport *Arg* 4D **27**
Isle of Skye Airstrip *High* 3F **63**
Isle of Whithorn *Dum* 4F **5**
Isleornsay *High* 4A **64**
Islesburgh *Shet* 5F **101**
Islesteps *Dum* 4E **13**
Islibhig *W Isl* 4A **96**
Itlaw *Abers* 4B **80**
Ivegill *Cumb* 3D **9**
Iverchaolain *Arg* 2E **29**

J

Jackton *S Lan* 4D **31**
Jamestown *Dum* 2C **14**
Jamestown *Fife* 1D **33**
Jamestown *High* 4B **76**
Jamestown *W Dun* 1B **30**
Janetstown *High* 1F **89** (nr Thurso)
Janetstown *High* 2C **90** (nr Wick)
Jedburgh *Bord* 3F **23**
Jemimaville *High* 3E **77**
Jenkins Park *High* 1A **56**
Johnby *Cumb* 4D **9**
John o' Groats *High* 5B **98**
Johnshaven *Abers* 4C **60**
Johnstone *Ren* 3C **30**
Johnstonebridge *Dum* 2F **13**
Joppa *Edin* 2F **33**
Joppa *S Ayr* 4F **19**
Juniper Green *Edin* 3D **33**
Jura Airstrip *Arg* 2F **27**

K

Kaimend *S Lan* 1E **21**
Kaimes *Edin* 3E **33**
Kaimrig End *Bord* 1F **21**
Kames *Arg* 2D **29**
Kames *E Ayr* 3B **20**
Kearvaig *High* 1D **87**
Kedlock Feus *Fife* 2C **42**
Keig *Abers* 4B **70**
Keilarsbrae *Clac* 4D **41**
Keillmore *Arg* 1A **28**
Keillor *Per* 3B **50**
Keillour *Per* 1E **41**
Keills *Arg* 3E **27**
Keiloch *Abers* 2C **58**
Keils *Arg* 3F **27**
Keir Mill *Dum* 2D **13**
Keisley *Cumb* 4F **9**
Keiss *High* 1C **90**
Keith *Mor* 4F **79**
Keith Inch *Abers* 1F **71**
Kellan *Arg* 3C **44**
Kellas *Ang* 4D **51**
Kellas *Mor* 4C **78**
Kelloholm *Dum* 4C **20**
Kelsick *Cumb* 2A **8**
Kelso *Bord* 2A **24**
Keltneyburn *Per* 3C **48**
Kelton *Dum* 4E **13**
Kelton Hill *Dum* 2C **6**
Kelty *Fife* 4A **42**
Kelvinside *Glas* 3D **31**
Kemback *Fife* 2D **43**
Kemnay *Abers* 4C **70**
Kengharair *Arg* 3B **44**
Kenknock *Stir* 4F **47**
Kenmore *High* 4A **74**
Kenmore *Per* 3C **48**
Kennacraig *Arg* 3C **28**
Kennet *Clac* 4E **41**
Kennethmont *Abers* 3A **70**
Kennoway *Fife* 3C **42**
Kenovay *Arg* 3E **91**
Kensaleyre *High* 4D **73**
Kentallen *High* 2B **46**
Kentra *High* 1D **45**
Keoldale *High* 1E **87**
Keppoch *High* 3C **64**
Kerrow *High* 2A **66**
Kerrycroy *Arg* 3F **29**
Kerse *Ren* 4B **30**
Kershopefoot *Cumb* 3D **15**
Keswick *Cumb* 4B **8**
Kettins *Per* 4B **50**
Kettlebridge *Fife* 3C **42**
Kettleholm *Dum* 4A **14**
Kettletoft *Orkn* 4H **99**
Keyhead *Abers* 4F **81**
Kiel Crofts *Arg* 4A **46**
Kielder *Nmbd* 2F **15**
Kilbagie *Fife* 4E **41**
Kilbarchan *Ren* 3C **30**
Kilbeg *High* 1F **53**
Kilberry *Arg* 3B **28**
Kilbirnie *N Ayr* 4B **30**
Kilbride *Arg* 1F **37**
Kilbride *High* 3E **63**
Kilbucho Place *Bord* 2F **21**
Kilchattan *Arg* 4A **36**
Kilchattan Bay *Arg* 4F **29**
Kilchenzie *Arg* 3D **17**
Kilcheran *Arg* 4F **45**
Kilchiaran *Arg* 3C **26**
Kilchoan *High* 2A **54** (nr Inverie)
Kilchoan *High* 1B **44** (nr Tobermory)
Kilchoman *Arg* 3C **26**
Kilchrenan *Arg* 1B **38**
Kilconquhar *Fife* 3D **43**
Kilcoy *High* 4C **76**
Kilcreggan *Arg* 1A **30**
Kildary *High* 2E **77**
Kildermorie Lodge *High* 2C **76**
Kildonan *High* 1E **85** (nr Helmsdale)
Kildonan *High* 4C **72** (nr Isle of Skye)
Kildonan *Dum* 2B **4**
Kildonan *N Ayr* 3B **18**
Kildonnan *High* 3D **53**
Kildrummy *Abers* 4F **69**
Kilfillan *Dum* 2D **5**
Kilfinan *Arg* 2D **29**
Kilfinnan *High* 2F **55**
Kilgour *Fife* 3B **42**
Kilgrammie *S Ayr* 1D **11**
Kilham *Nmbd* 2B **24**
Kilkenneth *Arg* 3E **91**
Killandrist *Arg* 3F **45**
Killean *Arg* 1D **17**
Killearn *Stir* 1D **31**
Killellan *Arg* 4D **17**
Killen *High* 4D **77**
Killichonan *Per* 2A **48**
Killiechronan *Arg* 3C **44**
Killiecrankie *Per* 1E **49**
Killilan *High* 2C **64**
Killimster *High* 2C **90**
Killin *Stir* 4A **48**
Killin Lodge *High* 1C **56**
Killinochonoch *Arg* 4F **37**
Killochyett *Bord* 1D **23**
Killundine *High* 3C **44**
Kilmacolm *Inv* 3B **30**
Kilmahog *Stir* 3B **40**
Kilmahumaig *Arg* 4E **37**
Kilmalieu *High* 2F **45**
Kilmaluag *High* 2D **73**
Kilmany *Fife* 1C **42**
Kilmarie *High* 4E **63**
Kilmarnock *E Ayr* **106** (2F **19**)
Kilmaron *Fife* 2C **42**
Kilmartin *Arg* 4F **37**
Kilmaurs *E Ayr* 1F **19**
Kilmelford *Arg* 2F **37**
Kilmeny *Arg* 3D **27**
Kilmichael Glassary *Arg* 4F **37**
Kilmichael of Inverlussa *Arg* 1B **28**
Kilmoluaig *Arg* 3E **91**
Kilmorack *High* 1B **66**
Kilmore *Arg* 1F **37**
Kilmore *High* 1F **53**
Kilmory *High* 4E **53** (nr Kilchoan)
Kilmory *High* 1C **52** (nr Rùm)
Kilmory *Arg* 2B **28**
Kilmory *N Ayr* 3A **18**
Kilmory Lodge *Arg* 3E **37**
Kilmote *High* 2E **85**
Kilmuir *High* 1B **62** (nr Dunvegan)
Kilmuir *High* 2E **77** (nr Invergordon)
Kilmuir *High* 1D **67** (nr Inverness)
Kilmuir *High* 2C **72** (nr Uig)
Kilmun *Arg* 1F **29**
Kilnave *Arg* 2C **26**
Kilncadzow *S Lan* 1D **21**
Kilnhill *Cumb* 4B **8**
Kilninian *Arg* 3A **44**
Kilninver *Arg* 1F **37**
Kiloran *Arg* 4A **36**
Kilpatrick *N Ayr* 3A **18**
Kilrenny *Fife* 3E **43**
Kilspindie *Per* 1B **42**
Kilsyth *N Lan* 2F **31**
Kiltarlity *High* 1C **66**
Kilvaxter *High* 3C **72**
Kilwinning *N Ayr* 1D **19**
Kimmerston *Nmbd* 2C **24**
Kinbeachie *High* 3D **77**
Kinbrace *High* 4D **89**
Kinbuck *Stir* 3D **40**
Kincaple *Fife* 2D **43**
Kincardine *Fife* 1B **32**
Kincardine *High* 1D **77**
Kincardine O'Neil *Abers* 2A **60**
Kinchrackine *Arg* 1C **38**
Kincorth *Aber* 1E **61**
Kincraig *High* 1F **57**
Kincraigie *Per* 3E **49**
Kindallachan *Per* 2E **49**
Kinfauns *Per* 1A **42**
Kingairloch *High* 2F **45**
Kingarth *Arg* 4E **29**
King Edward *Abers* 4C **80**
Kingholm Quay *Dum* 4E **13**
Kinghorn *Fife* 1E **33**
Kingie *High* 1E **55**
Kinglassie *Fife* 4B **42**
Kingledores *Bord* 3A **22**
King o' Muirs *Clac* 4D **41**
Kingoodie *Per* 1C **42**
Kingsbarns *Fife* 2E **43**
Kingsburgh *High* 4C **72**
Kingscavil *W Lot* 2C **32**
Kingscross *N Ayr* 3B **18**
Kingseat *Fife* 4A **42**
Kingsford *E Ayr* 1F **19**
Kingshouse *High* 2D **47**
Kingshouse *Stir* 1A **40**
Kingskettle *Fife* 3C **42**
Kings Muir *Bord* 2B **22**
Kingsmuir *Ang* 3D **51**
Kingsmuir *Fife* 3E **43**
Kingsteps *High* 4A **78**
Kingston *E Lot* 1B **34**
Kingston *Mor* 3E **79**
Kingswells *Aber* 1D **61**
Kingswood *Per* 4F **49**
Kingussie *High* 1E **57**
Kinharrachie *Abers* 2E **71**
Kinhrive *High* 2D **77**
Kinkell Bridge *Per* 2E **41**
Kinknockie *Abers* 1F **71**
Kinkry Hill *Cumb* 4E **15**
Kinloch *High* 4E **87** (nr Loch More)
Kinloch *High* 2D **45** (nr Lochaline)
Kinloch *High* 2C **52** (nr Rùm)
Kinloch *Per* 3A **50**
Kinlochard *Stir* 3F **39**
Kinlochbervie *High* 2D **87**
Kinlocheil *High* 4C **54**
Kinlochewe *High* 3D **75**
Kinloch Hourn *High* 1C **54**

Lower Oakfield – Newmains

Lower Oakfield *Fife* 4A 42
Lower Ollach *High* 2E 63
Lower Pitkerrie *High* 2F 77
Lowertown *Orkn* 3C 98
Low Hesket *Cumb* 3D 9
Lowick *Nmbd* 2D 25
Low Lorton *Cumb* 4A 8
Low Newton-by-the-Sea *Nmbd* 3F 25
Lownie Moor *Ang* 3D 51
Lowood *Bord* 2E 23
Low Row *Cumb* 1E 9 (nr Brampton)
Low Row *Cumb* 3A 8 (nr Wigton)
Low Torry *Fife* 1C 32
Low Valleyfield *Fife* 1B 32
Low Whinnow *Cumb* 2C 8
Lubcroy *High* 3E 83
Lubinvullin *High* 1A 88
Lucker *Nmbd* 2E 25
Lucklawhill *Fife* 1D 43
Ludag *W Isl* 1C 92
Lugar *E Ayr* 3A 20
Luggate Burn *E Lot* 2C 34
Luggiebank *N Lan* 2F 31
Lugton *E Ayr* 4C 30
Luib *High* 3E 63
Luib *Stir* 1F 39
Lumphanan *Abers* 1A 60
Lumphinnans *Fife* 4A 42
Lumsdaine *Bord* 3E 35
Lumsden *Abers* 3F 69
Lunan *Ang* 2F 51
Lunanhead *Ang* 2D 51
Luncarty *Per* 1F 41
Lundie *Ang* 4B 50
Lundin Links *Fife* 3D 43
Lunna *Shet* 5G 101
Lunning *Shet* 5H 101
Luss *Arg* 4E 39
Lussagiven *Arg* 1A 28
Lusta *High* 4B 72
Luthermuir *Abers* 1F 51
Luthrie *Fife* 2C 42
Lybster *High* 4B 90
Lyham *Nmbd* 2D 25
Lylestone *N Ayr* 1E 19
Lynaberack Lodge *High* 2E 57
Lynchat *High* 1E 57
Lyne *Bord* 1B 22
Lyneholmeford *Cumb* 4E 15
Lyne of Gorthleck *High* 3C 66
Lyne of Skene *Abers* 4C 70
Lyness *Orkn* 3B 98
Lynwilg *High* 4F 67
Lyth *High* 1B 90
Lythes *Orkn* 4C 98
Lythmore *High* 1F 89

M

Mabie *Dum* 4E 13
Macbiehill *Bord* 4D 33
Macduff *Abers* 3C 80
Machan *S Lan* 4F 31
Macharioch *Arg* 4E 17
Machrie *N Ayr* 2F 17
Machrihanish *Arg* 3D 17
Macmerry *E Lot* 2A 34
Madderty *Per* 1E 41
Maddiston *Falk* 2B 32
Maggieknockater *Mor* 1E 69
Maidens *S Ayr* 1D 11
Mail *Shet* 4C 100
Mains of Auchindachy *Mor* 1F 69
Mains of Auchnagatt *Abers* 1E 71
Mains of Drum *Abers* 2D 61
Mains of Edingight *Mor* 4A 80
Mainsriddle *Dum* 2E 7
Makerstoun *Bord* 2F 23
Malacleit *W Isl* 5B 94
Malaig *High* 2F 53
Malaig Bheag *High* 2F 53
Malcolmburn *Mor* 4E 79
Maligar *High* 3D 73
Mallaig *High* 2F 53
Malleny Mills *Edin* 3D 33
Malt Lane *Arg* 3B 38
Manais *W Isl* 4F 95
Mangurstadh *W Isl* 3B 96
Mannal *Arg* 3E 91
Mannerston *Falk* 2C 32
Mannofield *Aber* 1E 61
Mansewood *Glas* 3D 31
Mansfield *E Ayr* 4B 20
Maraig *W Isl* 2G 95
Marbhig *W Isl* 5F 97
Margnaheglish *N Ayr* 2B 18
Marishader *High* 3D 73
Marjoriebanks *Dum* 3F 13
Mark *Dum* 2C 4
Markethill *Per* 4B 50
Markinch *Fife* 3B 42
Mar Lodge *Abers* 3B 58
Marnoch *Abers* 4A 80
Marnock *N Lan* 3F 31
Marrel *High* 2F 85
Marrister *Shet* 5H 101
Marshall Meadows *Nmbd* 4F 35
Marwick *Orkn* 1A 98
Marybank *High* 4B 76 (nr Dingwall)
Marybank *High* 2E 77 (nr Invergordon)
Maryburgh *High* 4C 76
Maryhill *Glas* 3D 31
Marykirk *Abers* 1F 51
Marypark *Mor* 2C 68
Maryport *Cumb* 4F 7
Maryport *Dum* 4C 4
Maryton *Ang* 2C 50 (nr Kirriemuir)
Maryton *Ang* 2F 51 (nr Montrose)
Marywell *Abers* 2A 60
Marywell *Ang* 3F 51
Masons Lodge *Abers* 1D 61
Mastrick *Aber* 1E 61
Matterdale End *Cumb* 4C 8
Mauchline *E Ayr* 3F 19
Maud *Abers* 1E 71
Mawbray *Cumb* 3F 7
Maxton *Bord* 2F 23
Maxwellheugh *Bord* 2A 24
Maxwelltown *Dum* 4E 13
Maybole *S Ayr* 4E 19
Mayfield *Midl* 3F 33
Mayfield *Per* 1F 41
Maywick *Shet* 4B 100
Meadowmill *E Lot* 2A 34
Mealabost *W Isl* 1F 97 (nr Borgh)
Mealabost *W Isl* 3F 97 (nr Stornoway)
Mealasta *W Isl* 4A 96
Mealrigg *Cumb* 3A 8
Mealsgate *Cumb* 3B 8
Meigle *Per* 3B 50
Meikle Earnock *S Lan* 4F 31
Meikle Kilchattan Butts *Arg* 4E 29
Meikleour *Per* 4A 50
Meikle Tarty *Abers* 3E 71
Meikle Wartle *Abers* 2C 70
Melby *Shet* 1A 100
Melfort *Arg* 2F 37
Melgarve *High* 2B 56
Melkington *Nmbd* 1B 24
Melkinthorpe *Cumb* 4E 9
Melkridge *Nmbd* 1F 9
Mellangaun *High* 1B 74
Melldalloch *Arg* 2D 29
Mellguards *Cumb* 3D 9
Mellon Charles *High* 1B 74
Mellon Udrigle *High* 1B 74
Melmerby *Cumb* 4F 9
Melrose *Bord* 2E 23
Melsetter *Orkn* 4A 98
Melvaig *High* 1A 74
Melvich *High* 1D 89
Memsie *Abers* 3E 81
Memus *Ang* 2D 51
Mennock *Dum* 1D 13
Menstrie *Clac* 4D 41
Merchiston *Edin* 2E 33
Merkadale *High* 2C 62
Merkland *S Ayr* 2D 11
Merkland Lodge *High* 1E 83
Methil *Fife* 4C 42
Methilhill *Fife* 4C 42
Methlick *Abers* 2D 71
Methven *Per* 1F 41
Mey *High* 5A 98
Miabhag *W Isl* 3F 95 (nr Tarbert)
Miabhaig *W Isl* 2E 95 (nr Cliasmol)
Miabhaig *W Isl* 3B 96 (nr Timsgearraidh)
Mial *High* 2A 74
Micklethwaite *Cumb* 2B 8
Mid Ardlaw *Abers* 3E 81
Midbea *Orkn* 3F 99
Mid Beltie *Abers* 1B 60
Mid Calder *W Lot* 3C 32
Mid Clyth *High* 4B 90
Middlebie *Dum* 4B 14
Middle Drums *Ang* 2E 51
Middle Essie *Abers* 4F 81
Middlemuir *Abers* 1D 71 (nr New Deer)
Middlemuir *Abers* 4E 81 (nr Strichen)
Middlesceugh *Cumb* 3C 8
Middleton *Nmbd* 2E 25
Middleton *Ang* 3E 51
Middleton *Arg* 3E 91
Middleton *Midl* 4F 33
Middleton *Per* 3A 42
Midfield *High* 1A 88
Mid Garrary *Dum* 4A 12
Midgeholme *Cumb* 2F 9
Mid Ho *Shet* 2H 101
Mid Kirkton *N Ayr* 4F 29
Midland *Orkn* 2B 98
Midlem *Bord* 3E 23
Midton *Inv* 2A 30
Midtown *High* 1B 74 (nr Poolewe)
Midtown *High* 1A 88 (nr Tongue)
Mid Walls *Shet* 2A 100
Mid Yell *Shet* 2H 101
Migdale *High* 4B 84
Migvie *Abers* 1F 59
Milburn *Cumb* 4F 9
Milesmark *Fife* 1C 32
Milfield *Nmbd* 2C 24
Millbank *High* 1A 90
Millbeck *Cumb* 4B 8
Millbounds *Orkn* 4G 99
Millbreck *Abers* 1F 71
Millden Lodge *Ang* 4A 60
Milldens *Ang* 2E 51
Millearn *Per* 2E 41
Millerhill *Midl* 3F 33
Millerston *Glas* 3E 31
Millfield *Abers* 2F 59
Millhall *E Ren* 4D 31
Millheugh *S Lan* 4F 31
Millhouse *Arg* 2D 29
Millhouse *Cumb* 4C 8
Millhousebridge *Dum* 3A 14
Millikenpark *Ren* 3C 30
Mill Knowe *Arg* 3E 17
Mill of Craigievar *Abers* 4A 70
Mill of Fintray *Abers* 4D 71
Mill of Haldane *W Dun* 1C 30
Millport *N Ayr* 4F 29
Milltimber *Aber* 1D 61
Milltown *Abers* 1D 59 (nr Corgarff)
Milltown *Abers* 4E 69 (nr Lumsden)
Milltown *Dum* 4C 14
Milltown of Aberdalgie *Per* 1F 41
Milltown of Auchindoun *Mor* 1E 69
Milltown of Campfield *Abers* 1B 60
Milltown of Edinvillie *Mor* 1D 69
Milltown of Rothiemay *Mor* 1A 70
Milltown of Towie *Abers* 4F 69
Milnacraig *Ang* 2B 50
Milnathort *Per* 3A 42
Milngavie *E Dun* 2D 31
Milnholm *Stir* 1F 31
Milton *Cumb* 1E 9 (nr Brampton)
Milton *Dum* 4D 13 (nr Crocketford)
Milton *Dum* 2D 5 (nr Glenluce)
Milton *High* 4A 76 (nr Achnasheen)
Milton *High* 1A 64 (nr Applecross)
Milton *High* 2B 66 (nr Drumnadrochit)
Milton *High* 2E 77 (nr Invergordon)
Milton *High* 1C 66 (nr Inverness)
Milton *High* 2C 90 (nr Wick)
Milton *Mor* 3A 80 (nr Cullen)
Milton *Mor* 4C 68 (nr Tomintoul)
Milton *Stir* 3A 40 (nr Aberfoyle)
Milton *Stir* 4F 39 (nr Drymen)
Milton *Ang* 3C 50
Milton *Glas* 3D 31
Milton *S Ayr* 3F 19
Milton *W Dun* 2C 30
Milton Auchlossan *Abers* 1A 60
Milton Bridge *Midl* 3E 33
Milton Coldwells *Abers* 2E 71
Miltonduff *Mor* 3C 78
Milton Morenish *Per* 4B 48
Milton of Auchinhove *Abers* 1A 60
Milton of Balgonie *Fife* 3C 42
Milton of Barras *Abers* 4D 61
Milton of Campsie *E Dun* 2E 31
Milton of Cultoquhey *Per* 1D 41
Milton of Cushnie *Abers* 4A 70
Milton of Finavon *Ang* 2D 51
Milton of Gollanfield *High* 4E 77
Milton of Lesmore *Abers* 3F 69
Milton of Leys *High* 1D 67
Milton of Tullich *Abers* 2E 59
Minard *Arg* 4A 38
Mindrum *Nmbd* 2B 24
Mingarrypark *High* 1D 45
Mingary *High* 1C 44
Mingearraidh *W Isl* 5G 93
Minishant *S Ayr* 4E 19
Minnigaff *Dum* 1F 5
Mintlaw *Abers* 1F 71
Minto *Bord* 3E 23
Miodar *Arg* 3F 91
Mirbister *Orkn* 5E 99
Mireland *High* 1C 90
Moaness *Orkn* 2A 98
Moarfield *Shet* 1H 101
Moat *Cumb* 4D 15
Mochrum *Dum* 3E 5
Modsarie *High* 1B 88
Moffat *Dum* 1F 13
Mol-chlach *High* 4D 63
Moll *High* 3E 63
Mollinsburn *N Lan* 2F 31
Monachyle *Stir* 2F 39
Monar Lodge *High* 1F 65
Moneydie *Per* 1F 41
Moniaive *Dum* 2C 12
Monifieth *Ang* 4E 51
Monikie *Ang* 4E 51
Monimail *Fife* 2B 42
Monkhill *Cumb* 2C 8
Monkshill *Abers* 1C 70
Monkton *S Ayr* 3E 19
Monktonhill *S Ayr* 3E 19
Monreith *Dum* 3E 5
Montford *Arg* 3F 29
Montgarrie *Abers* 4A 70
Montgarswood *E Ayr* 3A 20
Montgreenan *N Ayr* 1E 19
Montrave *Fife* 3C 42
Montrose *Ang* 2F 51
Monymusk *Abers* 4B 70
Monzie *Per* 1D 41
Moodiesburn *N Lan* 2E 31
Moonzie *Fife* 2C 42
Moorbrae *Shet* 3G 101
Moorend *Dum* 4B 14
Moorhouse *Cumb* 2C 8 (nr Carlisle)
Moorhouse *Cumb* 2B 8 (nr Wigton)
Moor of Granary *Mor* 4B 78
Moor Row *Cumb* 3B 8
Morangie *High* 1E 77
Morar *High* 2F 53
Morebattle *Bord* 3A 24
Morefield *High* 4C 82
Morenish *Per* 4A 48
Morham *E Lot* 2B 34
Morningside *Edin* 2E 33
Morningside *N Lan* 4A 32
Morrington *Dum* 3D 13
Morton *Cumb* 4D 9 (nr Calthwaite)
Morton *Cumb* 2C 8 (nr Carlisle)
Morvich *High* 3C 84 (nr Golspie)
Morvich *High* 3C 64 (nr Shiel Bridge)
Morwick *Nmbd* 4F 25
Moscow *E Ayr* 1F 19
Mosedale *Cumb* 4C 8
Moss *Arg* 3E 91
Moss *High* 1D 45
Mossatt *Abers* 4F 69
Mossbank *Shet* 4G 101
Mossblown *S Ayr* 3F 19
Mossburnford *Bord* 4F 23
Mossdale *Dum* 4B 12
Mossedge *Cumb* 1D 9
Mossend *N Lan* 3F 31
Moss of Barmuckity *Mor* 3D 79
Mosspark *Glas* 3D 31
Mosspaul *Bord* 2D 15
Moss Side *Cumb* 2A 8
Moss-side *High* 4F 77
Moss-side of Cairness *Abers* 3F 81
Mosstodloch *Mor* 3E 79
Motherby *Cumb* 4D 9
Motherwell *N Lan* 106 (4F 31)
Moulin *Per* 2E 49
Mountain Cross *Bord* 1A 22
Mountbenger *Bord* 3C 22
Mountblow *W Dun* 2C 30
Mountgerald *High* 3C 76
Mount High *High* 3D 77
Mount Lothian *Midl* 4E 33
Mount Stuart *Arg* 4F 29
Mouswald *Dum* 4F 13
Mowhaugh *Bord* 3B 24
Moy *High* 2E 67
Moy Lodge *High* 3B 56
Muasdale *Arg* 1D 17
Muchalls *Abers* 2E 61
Muchrachd *High* 2F 65
Muckle Breck *Shet* 5H 101
Mudale *High* 4A 88
Mugdock *Stir* 2D 31
Mugeary *High* 2D 63
Muie *High* 3B 84
Muirden *Abers* 4C 80
Muirdrum *Ang* 4E 51
Muiredge *Per* 1B 42
Muirend *Glas* 3D 31
Muirhead *N Lan* 3E 31
Muirhead *Ang* 4C 50
Muirhead *Fife* 3B 42
Muirhouses *Falk* 1C 32
Muirkirk *E Ayr* 3B 20
Muir of Alford *Abers* 4A 70
Muir of Fairburn *High* 4B 76
Muir of Fowlis *Abers* 4A 70
Muir of Miltonduff *Mor* 4C 78
Muir of Ord *High* 4C 76
Muir of Tarradale *High* 4C 76
Muirshearlich *High* 3E 55
Muirtack *Abers* 2E 71
Muirton *High* 3E 77
Muirton *Per* 1A 42
Muirton of Ardblair *Per* 3A 50
Muirtown *Per* 2E 41
Muiryfold *Abers* 4C 80
Mulben *Mor* 4E 79
Mulindry *Arg* 4D 27
Mulla *Shet* 5G 101
Mullach Charlabhaigh *W Isl* 2D 96
Munerigie *High* 1F 55
Muness *Shet* 1H 101
Mungasdale *High* 4A 82
Mungrisdale *Cumb* 4C 8
Munlochy *High* 4D 77
Murieston *W Lot* 3C 32
Murkle *High* 1A 90
Murlaggan *High* 2D 55
Murra *Orkn* 2A 98
Murray, The *S Lan* 4E 31
Murrayfield *Edin* 2E 33
Murroes *Ang* 4D 51
Murthly *Per* 4F 49
Murton *Nmbd* 1C 24
Musselburgh *E Lot* 2F 33
Mutehill *Dum* 3B 6
Muthill *Per* 2D 41
Mybster *High* 2A 90
Myrebird *Abers* 2C 60
Myrelandhorn *High* 2B 90

N

Naast *High* 1B 74
Na Buirgh *W Isl* 3E 95
Na Gearrannan *W Isl* 2C 96
Nairn *High* 4F 77
Navidale *High* 2F 85
Nealhouse *Cumb* 2C 8
Nedd *High* 4C 86
Neilston *E Ren* 4C 30
Nemphlar *S Lan* 1D 21
Nenthall *Cumb* 3F 9
Nenthorn *Bord* 2F 23
Neribus *Arg* 4C 26
Nerston *S Lan* 4E 31
Nesbit *Nmbd* 2C 24
Ness of Tenston *Orkn* 1A 98
Nethanfoot *S Lan* 1D 21
Nether Blainslie *Bord* 1E 23
Netherbrae *Abers* 4C 80
Netherbrough *Orkn* 1B 98
Netherburn *S Lan* 1D 21
Netherby *Cumb* 4C 14
Nether Careston *Ang* 2E 51
Nether Dallachy *Mor* 3E 79
Nether Durdie *Per* 1B 42
Nether Howcleugh *S Lan* 4F 21
Nether Kinmundy *Abers* 1F 71
Netherlaw *Dum* 3C 6
Netherley *Abers* 2D 61
Nethermill *Dum* 3F 13
Nethermills *Mor* 4A 80
Netherplace *E Ren* 4D 31
Netherthird *E Ayr* 4A 20
Netherton *Ang* 2E 51
Netherton *Cumb* 4F 7
Netherton *N Lan* 4F 31
Netherton *Nmbd* 4C 24
Netherton *Per* 2A 50
Netherton *Stir* 2D 31
Nethertown *High* 5B 98
Nether Urquhart *Fife* 3A 42
Nether Welton *Cumb* 3C 8
Nethy Bridge *High* 3B 68
Neuk, The *Abers* 2C 60
New Abbey *Dum* 1E 7
New Aberdour *Abers* 3D 81
New Alyth *Per* 3B 50
Newark *Orkn* 3H 99
Newarthill *N Lan* 4F 31
Newbattle *Midl* 3F 33
New Bewick *Nmbd* 3D 25
Newbie *Dum* 1A 8
Newbiggin *Cumb* 4F 9 (nr Appleby)
Newbiggin *Cumb* 3E 9 (nr Cumrew)
Newbiggin *Cumb* 4D 9 (nr Penrith)
Newbigging *Ang* 4D 51 (nr Monikie)
Newbigging *Ang* 3B 50 (nr Newtyle)
Newbigging *Ang* 4D 51 (nr Tealing)
Newbigging *Edin* 2D 33
Newbigging *S Lan* 1F 21
New Bridge *Dum* 4E 13
Newbridge *Edin* 2D 33
Newburgh *Abers* 3E 71
Newburgh *Fife* 2B 42
Newby East *Cumb* 2D 9
New Byth *Abers* 4D 81
Newby West *Cumb* 2C 8
Newcastleton *Bord* 3D 15
New Cowper *Cumb* 3A 8
Newcraighall *Edin* 2F 33
New Cumnock *E Ayr* 4B 20
New Deer *Abers* 1D 71
New Elgin *Mor* 3D 79
New Galloway *Dum* 4B 12
Newham *Nmbd* 3E 25
Newhaven *Edin* 2E 33
Newhouse *N Lan* 3F 31
Newington *Edin* 2E 33
New Kelso *High* 1C 64
New Lanark *S Lan* 1D 21
Newlandrig *Midl* 3F 33
Newlands *Cumb* 4C 8
Newlands *High* 1E 67
Newlands of Geise *High* 1F 89
Newlands of Tynet *Mor* 3E 79
New Langholm *Dum* 3C 14
New Leeds *Abers* 4E 81
Newlot *Orkn* 1D 98
New Luce *Dum* 1C 4
Newmachar *Abers* 4D 71
Newmains *N Lan* 4A 32

New Mains of Ury – Renwick

New Mains of Ury Abers 3D 61
Newmarket W Isl 3F 97
New Mill Abers 1C 70
Newmill Bord 4D 23
Newmill Mor 4F 79
Newmills Fife 1C 32
Newmills High 3D 77
Newmiln Per 4A 50
Newmilns E Ayr 2A 20
Newmore High 4C 76
(nr Dingwall)
Newmore High 2D 77
(nr Invergordon)
Newpark Fife 2D 43
New Pitsligo Abers 4D 81
Newport High 1F 85
Newport-on-Tay Fife 1D 43
New Prestwick S Ayr 3E 19
New Rent Cumb 4D 9
New Sauchie Clac 4D 41
Newseat Abers 2C 70
New Shoreston Nmbd 2E 25
Newstead Bord 2E 23
New Stevenston N Lan 4F 31
Newton Dum 4B 14
(nr Annan)
Newton Dum 2A 14
(nr Moffat)
Newton High 3E 77
(nr Cromarty)
Newton High 1E 67
(nr Inverness)
Newton High 4D 87
(nr Kylestrome)
Newton High 3C 90
(nr Wick)
Newton S Lan 3E 31
(nr Glasgow)
Newton S Lan 2E 21
(nr Lanark)
Newton Arg 4B 38
Newton Bord 3F 23
Newton Mor 3C 78
Newton Shet 3B 100
Newton W Lot 2C 32
Newtonairds Dum 3D 13
Newton Arlosh Cumb 2B 8
Newtongrange Midl 3F 33
Newtonhill Abers 2E 61
Newtonhill High 1C 66
Newton Mearns E Ren 4D 31
Newtonmore High 2E 57
Newton of Ardtoe High 4F 53
Newton of Balcanquhal Per 2A 42
Newton of Beltrees Ren 4B 30
Newton of Falkland Fife 3B 42
Newton of Mountblairy Abers 4B 80
Newton of Pitcairns Per 2F 41
Newton on the Moor Nmbd 4E 25
Newton Reigny Cumb 4D 9
Newton Rigg Cumb 4D 9
Newton Stewart Dum 1F 5
Newton upon Ayr S Ayr 3E 19
New Town E Lot 2A 34
Newtown Cumb 3F 7
(nr Aspatria)
Newtown Cumb 1E 9
(nr Brampton)
Newtown Cumb 4E 9
(nr Penrith)
Newtown Nmbd 3D 25
Newtown Abers 3C 80
Newtown Falk 1B 32
Newtown High 1A 56
Newtown Shet 3G 101
Newtown St Boswells Bord 2E 23
Newtyle Ang 3B 50
New Winton E Lot 2A 34
Niddrie Edin 2F 33
Niddry W Lot 2C 32
Nigg Aber 1E 61
Nigg High 2F 77
Nigg Ferry High 3E 77
Ninemile Bar Dum 4D 13
Nine Mile Burn Midl 4D 33
Nisbet Bord 3F 23
Nisbet Hill Bord 4D 35
Nitshill Glas 3D 31
Noness Shet 4C 100
Nonikiln High 2D 77
Nook Cumb 4D 15
Noranside Ang 1D 51
Norby Shet 1A 100
Norham Nmbd 1C 24
North Balfern Dum 2F 5
North Ballachulish High 1B 46
North Berwick E Lot 1B 34
North Charlton Nmbd 3E 25
North Collafirth Shet 3F 101
North Commonty Abers 1D 71
North Craigo Ang 1F 51
North Dronley Ang 4C 50
Northdyke Orkn 1A 98
North Erradale High 1A 74
North Fearns High 2E 63
North Feorline N Ayr 3A 18
Northfield Aber 1D 61
North Gluss Shet 4F 101
North Hazelrigg Nmbd 2D 25
North Kessock High 1D 67
North Middleton Midl 4F 33
North Middleton Nmbd 3D 25
Northmuir Ang 2C 50
North Murie Per 1B 42
North Ness Orkn 3B 98
North Port Arg 1B 38
North Queensferry Fife 1D 33
North Roe Shet 3F 101
North Ronaldsay Airport Orkn 2H 99
North Row Cumb 4B 8
North Sannox N Ayr 1B 18
North Shian Arg 3A 46
North Side Cumb 4F 7
North Sunderland Nmbd 2F 25
North Town Shet 5B 100
Northtown Orkn 3C 98
Northwall Orkn 3H 99
North Water Bridge Ang 1F 51
North Watten High 2B 90
Norwick Shet 1H 101
Noss Shet 5B 100
Nostie High 3B 64
Nunclose Cumb 3D 9
Nunnerie S Lan 4E 21
Nybster High 1C 90

O

Oakbank Arg 4E 45
Oakbank W Lot 3C 32
Oakley Fife 1C 32
Oakshaw Ford Cumb 4E 15
Oape High 3F 83
Oathlaw Ang 2D 51
Oban Arg 106 (1F 37)
Oban W Isl 2F 95
Obsdale High 3D 77
Ochiltree E Ayr 3A 20
Ochtermuthill Per 2D 41
Ochtertyre Per 1D 41
Ockle High 4E 53
Octofad Arg 4C 26
Octomore Arg 4C 26
Oddsta Shet 2H 101
Odie Orkn 5H 99
Okraquoy Shet 3C 100
Old Aberdeen Aber 1E 61
Oldany High 4C 86
Old Bewick Nmbd 3D 25
Old Blair Per 1D 49
Old Bridge of Tilt Per 1D 49
Old Bridge of Urr Dum 1C 6
Old Dailly S Ayr 2D 11
Old Deer Abers 1E 71
Old Graitney Dum 1C 8
Oldhall High 2B 90
Oldhamstocks E Lot 2D 35
Old Kilpatrick W Dun 2C 30
Old Kinnernie Abers 1C 60
Oldmeldrum Abers 3D 71
Old Monkland N Lan 3F 31
Old Pentland Midl 3E 33
Old Philpstoun W Lot 2C 32
Old Rayne Abers 3B 70
Old Scone Per 1A 42
Oldshore Beg High 2C 86
Oldshoremore High 2D 87
Old Town Cumb 3D 9
Oldtown High 1C 76
Oldwall Cumb 1D 9
Old Westhall Abers 3B 70
Oldwhat Abers 4D 81
Olgrinmore High 2F 89
Ollaberry Shet 3F 101
Olrig High 1A 90
Omunsgarth Shet 2B 100
Onich High 1B 46
Onthank E Ayr 2F 19
Opinan High 2A 74
(nr Gairloch)
Opinan High 4A 82
(nr Laide)
Orasaigh W Isl 1H 95
Orbost High 1B 62
Ord High 4F 63
Ordale Shet 1H 101
Ordhead Abers 4B 70
Ordie Abers 1F 59
Ordiquish Mor 4E 79
Orgil Orkn 2A 98
Ormacleit W Isl 4G 93
Ormathwaite Cumb 4B 8
Ormiscaig High 1B 74
Ormiston E Lot 3A 34
Ormsaigbeg High 1B 44
Ormsaigmore High 1B 44
Ormsary Arg 2B 28
Orphir Orkn 2B 98
Orthwaite Cumb 4B 8
Orton Mor 4E 79
Osclay High 4B 90
Ose High 1C 62
Oskaig High 2E 63
Oskamull Arg 4B 44
Osmondwall Orkn 4B 98
Osnaburgh Fife 2D 43
Ospisdale High 1E 77
Otter Ferry Arg 1D 29
Otterswick Shet 3H 101
Oughterby Cumb 2B 8
Oughterside Cumb 3A 8
Oulton Cumb 2B 8
Ousby Cumb 4F 9
Ousdale High 2F 85
Outertown Orkn 1A 98
Overbister Orkn 3H 99
Over Finlarg Ang 3D 51
Overscaig High 1F 83
Overton Aber 4D 71
Overton High 4B 90
Overtown N Lan 4A 32
Oxgangs Edin 3E 33
Oxnam Bord 4A 24
Oxton Bord 4A 34
Oykel Bridge High 3E 83
Oyne Abers 3B 70

P

Pabail Iarach W Isl 3G 97
Pabail Uarach W Isl 3G 97
Padanaram Ang 2D 51
Paddockhole Dum 3B 14
Paibeil W Isl 1G 93
(nr North Uist)
Paibeil W Isl 3E 95
(nr Taransay)
Paiblesgearraidh W Isl 1G 93
Pairc Shiaboist W Isl 2D 96
Paisley Ren 107 (3C 30)
Palgowan Dum 3E 11
Palnackie Dum 2D 7
Palnure Dum 1F 5
Panbride Ang 4E 51
Pannanich Abers 2E 59
Papa Stour Airport Shet 1A 100
Papa Westray Airport Orkn 2F 99
Papcastle Cumb 4A 8
Papigoe High 2C 90
Papil Shet 3B 100
Papple E Lot 2B 34
Pardshaw Cumb 4F 7
Park Abers 2C 60
Park Arg 3A 46
Park Dum 2E 13
Parkburn Abers 2C 70
Parkgate Cumb 3B 8
Parkgate Dum 3F 13
Parkhall W Dun 2C 30
Parkhead Cumb 3C 8
Parkhead Glas 3E 31
Parkneuk Abers 4C 60
Parkside N Lan 4A 32
Park Village Nmbd 1F 9
Parsonby Cumb 4A 8
Partick Glas 3D 31
Parton Cumb 2B 8
Parton Dum 4B 12
Pathhead Abers 1F 51
Pathhead E Ayr 4B 20
Pathhead Fife 4B 42
Pathhead Midl 3F 33
Path of Condie Per 2F 41
Pathstruie Per 2F 41
Patna E Ayr 4F 19
Pattiesmuir Fife 1C 32
Pawston Nmbd 2B 24
Paxton Bord 4F 35
Pearsie Ang 2C 50
Peaston E Lot 3A 34
Peastonbank E Lot 3A 34
Peathill Abers 3E 81
Peat Inn Fife 3D 43
Peaton Arg 1A 30
Peebles Bord 1B 22
Peel Bord 2D 23
Peinchorran High 2E 63
Peinlich High 4D 73
Pelutho Cumb 3A 8
Pencaitland E Lot 3A 34
Penicuik Midl 3E 33
Penifiler High 1D 63
Peninver Arg 3E 17
Penkill S Ayr 2D 11
Pennan Abers 3D 81
Pennyghael Arg 1C 36
Pennyvenie E Ayr 1F 11
Penpont Dum 2D 13
Penrith Cumb 4E 9
Penruddock Cumb 4D 9
Penston E Lot 2A 34
Perceton N Ayr 1E 19
Percyhorner Abers 3E 81
Perth Per 107 (1A 42)
Peterburn High 1A 74
Peterculter Aber 1D 61
Peterhead Abers 1F 71
Petertown Orkn 2B 98
Pettinain S Lan 1E 21
Pettycur Fife 1E 33
Philiphaugh Bord 3D 23
Philpstoun W Lot 2C 32
Pickletillem Fife 1D 43
Pierowall Orkn 3F 99
Pilton Edin 2E 33
Pinkerton E Lot 2D 35
Pinmore S Ayr 2D 11
Pinwherry S Ayr 3C 10
Piperhill High 4F 77
Pirnmill N Ayr 1F 17
Pisgah Stir 3C 40
Pitagowan Per 1D 49
Pitcairn Per 2D 49
Pitcairngreen Per 1F 41
Pitcalnie High 2F 77
Pitcaple Abers 3C 70
Pitcox E Lot 2C 34
Pitcur Per 4B 50
Pitfichie Abers 4B 70
Pitgrudy High 4C 84
Pitkennedy Ang 2E 51
Pitlessie Fife 3C 42
Pitlochry Per 2E 49
Pitmachie Abers 3B 70
Pitmaduthy High 2E 77
Pitmedden Abers 3D 71
Pitnacree Per 2E 49
Pitroddie Per 1B 42
Pitscottie Fife 2D 43
Pittentrail High 3C 84
Pittenweem Fife 3E 43
Pittulie Abers 3E 81
Pitversie Per 2A 42
Plaidy Abers 4C 80
Plains N Lan 3F 31
Plean Stir 1A 32
Plenmeller Nmbd 1F 9
Plockton High 2B 64
Plocrapol W Isl 3F 95
Plumbland Cumb 4A 8
Plumpton Cumb 4D 9
Plumptonfoot Cumb 4D 9
Plumpton Head Cumb 4E 9
Polbae Dum 4D 11
Polbain High 3B 82
Polbeth W Lot 3C 32
Polchar High 1F 57
Poles High 4C 84
Polglass High 3B 82
Polio High 2E 77
Polla High 2E 87
Polloch High 1E 45
Pollok Glas 3D 31
Pollokshaws Glas 3D 31
Pollokshields Glas 3D 31
Polmaily High 2B 66
Polmont Falk 2B 32
Polnessan E Ayr 4F 19
Polnish High 3A 54
Polskeoch Dum 1B 12
Polton Midl 3E 33
Polwarth Bord 4D 35
Ponton Shet 1B 100
Poolewe High 1B 74
Pooley Bridge Cumb 4D 9
Pool o' Muckhart Clac 3F 41
Porin High 4A 76
Portachoillan Arg 4B 28
Port Adhair Bheinn na Faoghla W Isl 2G 93
Port Adhair Thirlodh Arg 3F 91
Port Ann Arg 1D 29
Port Appin Arg 3A 46
Port Asgaig Arg 3E 27
Port Askaig Arg 3E 27
Portavadie Arg 3D 29
Port Bannatyne Arg 3E 29
Port Carlisle Cumb 1B 8
Port Charlotte Arg 4C 26
Port Driseach Arg 2D 29
Port Dundas Glas 3D 31
Port Ellen Arg 1A 16
Port Elphinstone Abers 3C 70
Portencalzie Dum 4B 10
Portencross N Ayr 1C 18
Port Erroll Abers 2F 71
Portessie Mor 3F 79
Port Glasgow Inv 2B 30
Portgordon Mor 3E 79
Portgower High 2F 85
Port Henderson High 2A 74
Portincaple Arg 4D 39
Portinnisherrich Arg 2A 38
Portinscale Cumb 4B 8
Portknockie Mor 3F 79
Port Lamont Arg 2E 29
Portlethen Abers 2E 61
Portlethen Village Abers 2E 61
Portling Dum 2D 7
Port Logan Dum 3B 4
Portmahomack High 1A 78
Port Mholair W Isl 3G 97
Port Mor High 4D 53
Portnacroish Arg 3A 46
Portnahaven Arg 4B 26
Portnalong High 2C 62
Portnaluchaig High 3F 53
Portnancon High 1F 87
Port Nan Giuran W Isl 3G 97
Port nan Long W Isl 5C 94
Port Nis W Isl 1G 97
Portobello Edin 2F 33
Port of Menteith Stir 3A 40
Portormin High 4A 90
Portpatrick Dum 2B 4
Port Ramsay Arg 3F 45
Portree High 1D 63
Port Righ High 1D 63
Port Seton E Lot 2A 34
Portskerra High 1D 89
Portsonachan Arg 1B 38
Portsoy Abers 3A 80
Porttannachy Mor 3E 79
Portuairk High 1B 44
Port Wemyss Arg 4B 26
Port William Dum 3E 5
Potarch Abers 2B 60
Potterton Abers 4E 71
Poundland S Ayr 3C 10
Powburn Nmbd 4D 25
Powfoot Dum 1A 8
Powmill Per 4F 41
Prendwick Nmbd 4D 25
Pressen Nmbd 2B 24
Preston E Lot 2B 34
(nr East Linton)
Preston E Lot 2F 33
(nr Prestonpans)
Preston Bord 4D 35
Preston Nmbd 3E 25
Prestonmill Dum 2E 7
Prestonpans E Lot 2F 33
Prestwick S Ayr 3E 19
Priesthill Glas 3D 31
Priestland E Ayr 2A 20
Primsidemill Bord 3B 24
Prior Muir Fife 2E 43
Prospect Cumb 3A 8
Provanmill Glas 3E 31
Pulpit Hill Arg 1F 37
Pumpherston W Lot 3C 32

Q

Quarrier's Village Inv 3B 30
Quarrywood Mor 3C 78
Quartalehouse Abers 1E 71
Quarter N Ayr 3F 29
Quarter S Lan 4F 31
Queenzieburn N Lan 2E 31
Quendale Shet 5B 100
Quholm Orkn 1A 98
Quilquox Abers 2E 71
Quindry Orkn 3C 98
Quothquan S Lan 2E 21
Quoyloo Orkn 1A 98
Quoyness Orkn 2A 98
Quoys Shet 5G 101
(nr Mainland)
Quoys Shet 1H 101
(nr Unst)

R

Raby Cumb 2A 8
Rachan Mill Bord 2A 22
Racks Dum 4F 13
Rackwick Orkn 3A 98
(nr Hoy)
Rackwick Orkn 3F 99
(nr Westray)
Radernie Fife 3D 43
Rafford Mor 4B 78
Raggra High 3C 90
Raigbeg High 3F 67
Raise Cumb 3F 9
Rait Per 1B 42
Ralia High 2E 57
Ramasaig High 1A 62
Ramnageo Shet 1H 101
Ramsburn Mor 4A 80
Ramscraigs High 1F 85
Ramstone Abers 4B 70
Ranais W Isl 4F 97
Ranfurly Ren 3B 30
Rangag High 3A 90
Rankinston E Ayr 4F 19
Rannoch Station Per 2F 47
Ranochan High 3B 54
Raploch Stir 4C 40
Rapness Orkn 3G 99
Rascarrel Dum 3C 6
Rashfield Arg 1F 29
Ratagan High 4C 64
Rathen Abers 3F 81
Rathillet Fife 1C 42
Ratho Edin 2D 33
Ratho Station Edin 2D 33
Rathven Mor 3F 79
Rattar High 5A 98
Ratten Row Cumb 3C 8
Rattray Abers 4F 81
Rattray Per 3A 50
Raughton Cumb 3C 8
Raughton Head Cumb 3C 8
Ravenstruther S Lan 1E 21
Rearquhar High 4C 84
Reaster High 1B 90
Reawick Shet 2B 100
Reay High 1E 89
Rechullin High 4B 74
Redburn High 1A 68
Redcastle High 1C 66
Red Dial Cumb 3B 8
Redding Falk 2B 32
Reddingmuirhead Falk 2B 32
Redford Ang 3E 51
Redfordgreen Bord 4C 22
Redhill Abers 1C 60
Redhouses Arg 3D 27
Redland Orkn 5E 99
Redmain Cumb 4A 8
Redpath Bord 2E 23
Redpoint High 3A 74
Reemshill Abers 1C 70
Regoul High 4F 77
Reiff High 2A 82
Reinigeadal W Isl 2G 95
Reisque Abers 4D 71
Reiss High 2C 90
Relugas Mor 1A 68
Renfrew Ren 3D 31
Rennington Nmbd 4F 25
Renton W Dun 2B 30
Renwick Cumb 3E 9

Rescobie – Stonybreck

Rescobie Ang 2E 51
Resipole High 1E 45
Resolis High 3D 77
Rest and be thankful Arg 3D 39
Reston Bord 3E 35
Rheindown High 1C 66
Rhemore High 2C 44
Rhenetra High 4D 73
Rhian High 2A 84
Rhian Breck High 3A 84
Rhicarn High 1B 82
Rhiconich High 2D 87
Rhicullen High 2D 77
Rhidorroch High 4C 82
Rhifail High 3C 88
Rhilochan High 3C 84
Rhiroy High 1E 75
Rhitongue High 2B 88
Rhonehouse Dum 2C 6
Rhu Arg 1A 30
Rhubha Stoer High 4B 86
Rhubodach Arg 2E 29
Rhue High 4B 82
Rhunahaorine Arg 1E 17
Rhuvoult High 2D 87
Rhynd Per 1A 42
Rhynie Abers 3F 69
Ribigill High 2A 88
Riccarton E Ayr 2F 19
Rickarton Abers 3D 61
Rickerby Cumb 2D 9
Riemore Lodge Per 3F 49
Rigg Dum 1B 8
Riggend N Lan 2F 31
Rigside S Lan 2D 21
Rimsdale High 3C 88
Ringasta Shet 5B 100
Ringford Dum 2B 6
Rinmore Abers 4F 69
Rinnigill Orkn 3B 98
Riof W Isl 3C 96
Rireavach High 4B 82
Risabus Arg 1A 16
Rispond High 1F 87
Roadhead Cumb 4E 15
Roadmeetings S Lan 1D 21
Roadside High 1A 90
Roadside of Catterline Abers 4D 61
Roadside of Kinneff Abers 4D 61
Roag High 1B 62
Roberton Bord 4D 23
Roberton S Lan 3E 21
Robertstown Mor 1D 69
Rob Roy's House Arg 2C 38
Rock Nmbd 3F 25
Rockcliffe Cumb 1C 8
Rockcliffe Dum 2D 7
Rockcliffe Cross Cumb 1C 8
Rockfield High 1A 78
Roddam Nmbd 3D 25
Roddenloft E Ayr 3F 19
Rodel W Isl 4E 95
Roesound Shet 5F 101
Rogart High 3C 84
Romannobridge Bord 1A 22
Romesdal High 4D 73
Ronaldsvoe Orkn 3C 98
Rootfield High 4C 76
Rootpark S Lan 4B 32
Rora Abers 4F 81
Rorandle Abers 4B 70
Rosebank S Lan 1D 21
Roseden Nmbd 3D 25
Rosehall High 3F 83
Rosehearty Abers 3E 81
Roseisle Mor 3C 78
Rosemarkie High 4E 77
Rosemount Per 3A 50
Rosewell Midl 3E 33
Roshven High 4A 54
Roskhill High 1B 62
Rosley Cumb 3C 8
Roslin Midl 3E 33
Rosneath Arg 1A 30
Ross Bord 3F 35
Ross Dum 3B 6
Ross Nmbd 2E 25
Ross Per 1C 40
Rosskeen High 3D 77
Roster High 4B 90
Rosyth Fife 1D 33
Rothes Mor 1D 69
Rothesay Arg 3E 29
Rothienorman Abers 2C 70
Rothiesholm Orkn 5H 99
Rottal Ang 1C 50
Rough Haugh High 3C 88
Roughsike Cumb 4E 15
Roundyhill Ang 2C 50
Row Cumb 4F 9
Rowanburn Dum 4D 15
Rowanhill Abers 4F 81
Rowardennan Stir 4E 39
Rowfoot Nmbd 1F 9
Roxburgh Bord 2A 24
Roybridge High 3F 55
Ruaig Arg 3F 91
Ruarach High 3C 64
Ruchazie Glas 3E 31
Ruckcroft Cumb 3E 9
Ruglen S Ayr 1D 11
Ruilick High 1C 66
Ruisaurie High 1B 66
Ruisigearraidh W Isl 4D 94
Rumbling Bridge Per 4F 41
Rumford Falk 2B 32
Runtaleave Ang 1B 50
Ruskie Stir 3B 40
Russland Orkn 1B 98
Rutherglen S Lan 3E 31
Ruthrieston Aber 1E 61
Ruthven High 2F 67
(nr Inverness)
Ruthven High 2E 57
(nr Kingussie)
Ruthven Abers 1A 70
Ruthven Ang 3B 50
Ruthwaite Cumb 4B 8
Ruthwell Dum 1A 8
Rychraggan High 2B 66

S

Saasaig High 1F 53
Saddell Arg 2E 17
Saighdinis W Isl 1H 93
St Abbs Bord 3F 35
St Andrews Fife 107 (2E 43)
St Ann's Dum 2F 13
St Boswells Bord 2E 23
St Catherines Arg 3C 38
St Colmac Arg 3E 29
St Combs Abers 3F 81
St Cyrus Abers 1F 51
St David's Per 1E 41
St Fergus Abers 4F 81
St Fillans Per 1B 40
St Helens Cumb 4F 7
St John's Town of Dalry Dum 3B 12
St Katherines Abers 2C 70
St Madoes Per 1A 42
St Margaret's Hope Orkn 3C 98
St Martins Per 4A 50
St Mary's Orkn 2C 98
St Monans Fife 3E 43
St Ninians Stir 4C 40
St Quivox S Ayr 3E 19
St Vigeans Ang 3F 51
Salen Arg 3C 44
Salen High 1D 45
Saligo Arg 3C 26
Saline Fife 4F 41
Salkeld Dykes Cumb 4E 9
Sallachan High 1A 46
Sallachy High 3A 84
(nr Lairg)
Sallachy High 2C 64
(nr Stromeferry)
Salmond's Muir Ang 4E 51
Salsburgh N Lan 3A 32
Salta Cumb 3F 7
Saltburn High 3E 77
Saltcoats N Ayr 1D 19
Saltness Orkn 4A 98
Saltness Shet 2A 100
Salum Arg 3F 91
Samalaman High 4F 53
Samhia W Isl 1G 93
Samsonslane Orkn 5H 99
Samuelston E Lot 2A 34
Sanaigmore Arg 2C 26
Sand High 4A 82
Sand Shet 2B 100
Sandaig Arg 3E 91
Sandaig High 1A 54
Sandale Cumb 3B 8
Sandavore High 3D 53
Sanday Airport Orkn 3H 99
Sandbank Arg 1F 29
Sandend Abers 3A 80
Sandford S Lan 1C 20
Sandfordhill Abers 1F 71
Sandgreen Dum 2A 6
Sandhaven Abers 3E 81
Sandhead Dum 2B 4
Sandness Shet 1A 100
Sandsound Shet 2B 100
Sandvoe Shet 2F 101
Sandwick Orkn 1A 98
(nr Mainland)
Sandwick Orkn 4C 98
(nr South Ronaldsay)
Sandwick Shet 4C 100
(nr Mainland)
Sandwick Shet 5H 101
(nr Whalsay)
Sandyhills Dum 2D 7
Sandystones Bord 3E 23
Sangobeg High 1F 87
Sangomore High 1F 87
Sanna High 3B 44
Sanndabhaig W Isl 3F 97
(nr Isle of Lewis)
Sanndabhaig W Isl 3H 93
(nr South Uist)
Sannox N Ayr 1B 18
Sanquhar Dum 4C 20
Sarclet High 3C 90
Sauchen Abers 4B 70
Saucher Per 4A 50
Saughtree Bord 2E 15
Saval High 3A 84
Scadabhagh W Isl 3F 95
Scaladal W Isl 1F 95
Scalasaig Arg 4A 36
Scaleby Cumb 1D 9
Scalebyhill Cumb 1D 9
Scale Houses Cumb 3E 9
Scales Cumb 4C 8
Scalloway Shet 3C 100
Scalpaigh W Isl 3G 95
Scalpay House High 3F 63
Scamodale High 4B 54
Scaniport High 2D 67
Scapa Orkn 2C 98
Scar Orkn 3H 99
Scarasta W Isl 3E 95
Scardroy High 4F 75
Scarfskerry High 5A 98
Scarinish Arg 3F 91
Scarvister Shet 2B 100
Scatness Shet 5B 100
Scatwell High 4A 76
Scaur Dum 2D 7
Scolpaig W Isl 5B 94
Scone Per 1A 42
Sconser High 2E 63
Scoonie Fife 3C 42
Scoraig High 4B 82
Scotbheinn W Isl 2H 93
Scotby Cumb 2D 9
Scotlandwell Per 3A 42
Scotsburn High 2E 77
Scotsburn Mor 3D 79
Scotsdike Cumb 4C 14
Scotstoun Glas 3D 31
Scotstown High 1F 45
Scottas High 1A 54
Scourie High 3C 86
Scourie More High 3C 86
Scousburgh Shet 5B 100
Scrabster High 1F 89
Scrainwood Nmbd 4C 24
Scremerston Nmbd 1D 25
Scuggate Cumb 4D 15
Sculamus High 3F 63
Seafield High 1A 78
Seafield Midl 3E 33
Seafield S Ayr 3E 19
Seafield W Lot 3C 32
Seahouses Nmbd 2F 25
Seamill N Ayr 1D 19
Seaside Per 1B 42
Seater High 5B 98
Seaton Cumb 4F 7
Seatown Mor 3A 80
(nr Cullen)
Seatown Mor 2D 79
(nr Lossiemouth)
Seatown Abers 3A 80
Seaville Cumb 2A 8
Sebergham Cumb 3C 8
Second Coast High 4A 82
Sefster Shet 1B 100
Seggat Abers 1C 70
Seilebost W Isl 3E 95
Seisiadar W Isl 3G 97
Selkirk Bord 3D 23
Sellafirth Shet 2H 101
Semblister Shet 1B 100
Setter Shet 3G 101
Settiscarth Orkn 1B 98
Sgallairidh W Isl 3B 92
Sgarasta Mhor W Isl 3E 95
Sgiogarstaigh W Isl 1G 97
Sgreadan Arg 4A 36
Shandon Arg 1A 30
Shandwick High 2F 77
Shannochie N Ayr 3A 18
Sharperton Nmbd 4C 24
Shawhead Dum 4D 13
Shawwood E Ayr 3A 20
Shearington Dum 1F 7
Shebster High 1F 89
Sheddocksley Aber 1D 61
Shedog N Ayr 2A 18
Sheigra High 1C 86
Shennanton Dum 1E 5
Shenval Mor 3D 69
Sheppardstown High 3A 90
Sheriffston Mor 3D 79
Shettleston Glas 3E 31
Shiel Bridge High 4C 64
Shieldaig High 2B 74
(nr Charlestown)
Shieldaig High 4B 74
(nr Torridon)
Shieldhill Dum 3F 13
Shieldhill Falk 2A 32
Shieldhill S Lan 1F 21
Shieldmuir N Lan 4F 31
Shielfoot High 4F 53
Shielhill Abers 4F 81
Shielhill Ang 2D 51
Shilbottle Nmbd 4E 25
Shilbottle Grange Nmbd 4F 25
Shillford E Ren 4C 30
Shillmoor Nmbd 4B 24
Shinness High 2A 84
Shipley Nmbd 4E 25
Shire Cumb 4F 9
Shires Mill Fife 1C 32
Shiskine N Ayr 3A 18
Shopford Cumb 4E 15
Shoresdean Nmbd 1C 24
Shoreswood Nmbd 1C 24
Shotton Nmbd 2B 24
Shotts N Lan 3A 32
Shulishadermor High 1D 63
Shulista High 2D 73
Shurrery High 2F 89
Siabost W Isl 2D 96
Siabost bho Dheas W Isl 2D 96
Siabost bho Thuath W Isl 2D 96
Siadar W Isl 1E 97
Siadar Uarach W Isl 1E 97
Sibbaldbie Dum 3A 14
Sibster High 2C 90
Siddick Cumb 4F 7
Sighthill Edin 2D 33
Sildinis W Isl 1G 95
Silloth Cumb 2A 8
Sillyearn Mor 4A 80
Silverbank Abers 2C 60
Silverburn Midl 3E 33
Silverhillocks Abers 3C 80
Silverton W Dun 2C 30
Simprim Bord 1B 24
Sinclairston E Ayr 4F 19
Sinclairtown Fife 4B 42
Sinnahard Abers 4F 69
Skail High 3C 88
Skaill Orkn 1A 98
Skaills Orkn 2D 98
Skares E Ayr 4A 20
Skateraw E Lot 2D 35
Skaw Shet 5H 101
Skeabost High 1D 63
Skeabrae Orkn 1A 98
Skelberry Shet 5B 100
(nr Boddam)
Skelberry Shet 3F 101
(nr Housetter)
Skelbo High 4C 84
Skelbo Street High 4C 84
Skelfhill Bord 1D 15
Skellister Shet 1C 100
Skelmorlie N Ayr 3F 29
Skelpick High 2C 88
Skelton Cumb 4D 9
Skelwick Orkn 3F 99
Skeroblingarry Arg 3E 17
Skerray High 1B 88
Skerricha High 2D 87
Skiall High 1F 89
Skinburness Cumb 2A 8
Skinflats Falk 1B 32
Skinidin High 1B 62
Skinnet High 1A 88
Skipness Arg 4C 28
Skiprigg Cumb 3C 8
Skirling Bord 2F 21
Skirwith Cumb 4F 9
Skirza High 1C 90
Skitby Cumb 1D 9
Skroo Shet 1H 99
Skulamus High 3F 63
Skullomie High 1B 88
Skye of Curr High 3A 68
Slackhead Mor 3F 79
Slacks of Cairnbanno Abers 1D 71
Slaggyford Nmbd 2F 9
Slamannan Falk 2A 32
Slickly High 1B 90
Sliddery N Ayr 3A 18
Sligachan High 3D 63
Slochd High 3F 67
Slockavullin Arg 4F 37
Sluggan High 3F 67
Smailholm Bord 2F 23
Smallburn E Ayr 3B 20
Smallholm Dum 4A 14
Smeircleit W Isl 1C 92
Smerral High 4A 90
Smirisary High 4F 53
Smithfield Cumb 1D 9
Smithstown High 2A 74
Smithton High 1E 67
Smoogro Orkn 2B 98
Snaigow House Per 3F 49
Sniseabhal W Isl 4G 93
Sockbridge Cumb 4E 9
Sodom Shet 5H 101
Solas W Isl 5C 94
Sorbie Dum 3F 5
Sordale High 1A 90
Sorisdale Arg 1H 91
Sorn E Ayr 3A 20
Sornhill E Ayr 2A 20
Sortat High 1B 90
Soulby Cumb 4D 9
Sound Shet 2C 100
(nr Lerwick)
Sound Shet 1B 100
(nr Tresta)
Sourhope Bord 3B 24
Sourin Orkn 4F 99
Sour Nook Cumb 3C 8
South Alloa Falk 4D 41
Southannan N Ayr 4A 30
South Balfern Dum 2F 5
South Ballachulish High 2B 46
South Broomage Falk 1A 32
South Charlton Nmbd 3E 25
South Clunes High 1C 66
South Creagan Arg 3A 46
Southdean Bord 1F 15
Southend Arg 4D 17
Southerfield Cumb 3A 8
Southerhouse Shet 3B 100
Southerness Dum 2E 7
South Erradale High 2A 74
South Feorline N Ayr 3A 18
South Garvan High 4C 54
South Gluss Shet 4F 101
South Hazelrigg Nmbd 2D 25
South Kessock High 1D 67
South Kirkton Abers 1C 60
South Ledaig Arg 4A 46
South Middleton Nmbd 3C 24
South Newton N Ayr 4D 29
South Port Arg 1B 38
Southpunds Shet 5C 100
South Queensferry Edin 2D 33
Southside Orkn 5G 99
Southtown Orkn 3C 98
South View Shet 2B 100
Southwaite Cumb 3D 9
Soval Lodge W Isl 4E 97
Sowerby Row Cumb 3C 8
Soyal High 4A 84
Sparket Cumb 4D 9
Spean Bridge High 3F 55
Speybank High 1F 57
Spey Bay Mor 3E 79
Speybridge High 3B 68
Speyview Mor 1D 69
Spindlestone Nmbd 2E 25
Spinningdale High 1D 77
Spittal Dum 2E 5
Spittal E Lot 2A 34
Spittal High 2A 90
Spittal Nmbd 1D 25
Spittalfield Per 3A 50
Spittal of Glenmuick Abers 3E 59
Spittal of Glenshee Per 4C 58
Spittal-on-Rule Bord 3E 23
Spott E Lot 2C 34
Springburn Glas 3E 31
Springfield Dum 1C 8
Springfield Fife 2C 42
Springfield High 3D 77
Springholm Dum 1D 7
Springside N Ayr 2E 19
Sprouston Bord 2A 24
Sprunston Cumb 3D 9
Sraid Ruadh Arg 3E 91
Srannda W Isl 4E 95
Sron an t-Sithein High 1F 45
Sronphadruig Lodge Per 4E 57
Sruth Mor W Isl 1H 93
Stadhlaigearraidh W Isl 4G 93
Stafainn High 3D 73
Staffield Cumb 3E 9
Staffin High 3D 73
Stainburn Cumb 4F 7
Stainton Cumb 2C 8
(nr Carlisle)
Stainton Cumb 4D 9
(nr Penrith)
Stair E Ayr 3F 19
Stairhaven Dum 2D 5
Stamford Nmbd 4F 25
Stamperland E Ren 4D 31
Stand N Lan 3F 31
Standburn Falk 2B 32
Standingstone Cumb 3B 8
Stane N Lan 4A 32
Stanecastle N Ayr 2E 19
Stanhope Bord 3A 22
Stanley Per 4A 50
Stannersburn Nmbd 3F 15
Stanydale Shet 1A 100
Staoinebrig W Isl 4G 93
Stapleton Cumb 4E 15
Star Fife 3C 42
Staxigoe High 2C 90
Steelend Fife 4F 41
Steele Road Bord 2E 15
Stein High 4B 72
Steinmanhill Abers 1C 70
Stemster High 1A 90
(nr Halkirk)
Stemster High 1F 89
(nr Westfield)
Stenhouse Edin 2E 33
Stenhousemuir Falk 1A 32
Stenscholl High 3D 73
Stenso Orkn 5E 99
Stenton E Lot 2C 34
Steòrnabhagh W Isl 3F 97
Stepford Dum 3D 13
Stepps N Lan 3E 31
Stevenston N Ayr 1D 19
Stewarton Arg 4D 17
Stewarton E Ayr 1F 19
Stichill Bord 2A 24
Stirling Abers 1F 71
Stirling Stir 107 (4C 40)
Stittenham High 2D 77
Stobo Bord 2A 22
Stobo Castle Bord 2A 22
Stobs Castle Bord 1E 15
Stockdalewath Cumb 3C 8
Stoer High 1B 82
Stonebyres Holdings S Lan 1D 21
Stonefield Arg 4A 46
Stonefield S Lan 4E 31
Stonehaven Abers 3D 61
Stonehouse Nmbd 2F 9
Stonehouse S Lan 1C 20
Stoneyburn W Lot 3B 32
Stoneykirk Dum 2B 4
Stoneywood Aber 4D 71
Stonybreck Shet 1H 99

118 Scotland Regional Atlas

Stormontfield – West Culvennan

Stormontfield Per 1A 42
Stornoway W Isl 3F 97
Stornoway Airport W Isl 3F 97
Stotfield Mor 2D 79
Stoul High 2A 54
Stove Orkn 4H 99
Stove Shet 4C 100
Stow Bord 1D 23
Straad Arg 3E 29
Strachan Abers 2B 60
Straid S Ayr 2C 10
Straiton Midl 3E 33
Straiton S Ayr 1E 11
Straloch Per 1F 49
Stranraer Dum 1B 4
Strath High 2A 74
(nr Gairloch)
Strath High 2B 90
(nr Wick)
Strathan High 2C 54
(nr Fort William)
Strathan High 1B 82
(nr Lochinver)
Strathan High 1A 88
(nr Tongue)
Strathan Skerray High 1B 88
Strathaven S Lan 1C 20
Strathblane Stir 2D 31
Strathcanaird High 3C 82
Strathcarron High 1C 64
Strathcoil Arg 4D 45
Strathdon Abers 4E 69
Strathkinness Fife 2D 43
Strathmashie House High 2C 56
Strathmiglo Fife 2B 42
Strathmore Lodge High 3A 90
Strathpeffer High 4B 76
Strathrannoch High 2A 76
Strathtay Per 2E 49
Strathvaich Lodge High 2A 76
Strathwhillan N Ayr 2B 18
Strathy High 2D 77
(nr Invergordon)
Strathy High 1D 89
(nr Melvich)
Strathyre Stir 2A 40
Stravithie Fife 2E 43
Strichen Abers 4E 81
Stroanfreggan Dum 2B 12
Stromeferry High 2B 64
Stromemore High 2B 64
Stromness Orkn 2A 98
Stronachie Per 3F 41
Stronachlachar Stir 2F 39
Stronchreggan High 4D 55
Strone High 3C 66
(nr Drumnadrochit)
Strone High 1E 57
(nr Kingussie)
Strone Arg 1F 29
Stronenaba High 3F 55
Stronganess Shet 1H 101
Stronmilchan Arg 1C 38
Stronsay Airport Orkn 5H 99
Strontian High 1F 45
Struan High 2C 62
Struan Per 1D 49
Struanmore High 2C 62
Strutherhill S Lan 4F 31
Struy High 2B 66
Stuartfield Abers 1E 71
Suainebost W Isl 1G 97
Suardail W Isl 3F 97
Succoth Abers 2F 69
Succoth Arg 3D 39
Suisnish High 2E 63
Sulaisiadar W Isl 3G 97
Sùlaisiadar Mòr High 1D 63
Sullom Shet 4F 101
Sumburgh Shet 5C 100
Sumburgh Airport Shet 5B 100
Summerhill Aber 1E 61
Sunderland Cumb 4A 8
Sunnylaw Stir 4C 40
Sutors of Cromarty High 3F 77
Swanbister Orkn 2B 98
Swarister Shet 3H 101
Swiney High 4B 90
Swinhill S Lan 1C 20
Swinhoe Nmbd 3F 25
Swinister Shet 3F 101
Swinside Hall Bord 4A 24
Swinton Bord 1B 24
Swordale High 3C 76
Swordly High 1C 88
Symbister Shet 5H 101
Symington S Ayr 2E 19
Symington S Lan 2E 21
Syre High 3B 88

T

Tabost W Isl 1H 95
(nr Cearsiadar)
Tabost W Isl 1G 97
(nr Suainebost)
Tacleit W Isl 3C 96
Taigh a Ghearraidh W Isl 5B 94
Taigh Bhuirgh W Isl 3E 95
Tain High 1E 77
(nr Invergordon)
Tain High 1B 90
(nr Thurso)
Tairbeart W Isl 3F 95
Talisker High 2C 62
Talkin Cumb 2E 9
Talladale High 2C 74
Talla Linnfoots Bord 3A 22
Tallaminnock S Ayr 2E 11
Tallentire Cumb 4A 8
Talmine High 1A 88
Tandlehill Ren 3C 30
Tangasdal W Isl 2B 92
Tangwick Shet 4E 101
Tankerness Orkn 2D 98
Tannach High 3C 90
Tannadice Ang 2D 51
Tannochside N Lan 3F 31
Taobh a Chaolais W Isl 1C 92
Taobh a Deas Loch Aineort W Isl 5G 93
Taobh a Ghlinne W Isl 1H 95
Taobh a Tuath Loch Aineort W Isl 5G 93
Tarbert Arg 1A 28
(nr Jura)
Tarbert Arg 3C 28
(nr Kintyre)
Tarbert W Isl 3F 95
Tarbet High 2A 54
(nr Mallaig)
Tarbet High 3C 86
(nr Scourie)
Tarbet Arg 3E 39
Tarbolton S Ayr 3F 19
Tarbrax S Lan 4C 32
Tarfside Ang 4F 59
Tarland Abers 1F 59
Tarlogie High 1E 77
Tarns Cumb 3A 8
Tarrel High 1F 77
Tarsappie Per 1A 42
Tarscabhaig High 1E 53
Tarskavaig High 1E 53
Tarves Abers 2D 71
Tarvie High 4B 76
Tavool House Arg 1B 36
Tayinloan Arg 1D 17
Taynish Arg 1B 28
Taynuilt Arg 4B 46
Tayport Fife 1D 43
Tayvallich Arg 1B 28
Tealing Ang 4D 51
Teangue High 1F 53
Teanna Mhachair W Isl 1G 93
Tempar Per 2B 48
Templand Dum 3F 13
Temple Glas 3D 31
Temple Midl 4F 33
Templehall Fife 4B 42
Temple Sowerby Cumb 4F 9
Tenandry Per 1E 49
Tenga Arg 3C 44
Terregles Dum 4E 13
Teviothead Bord 1D 15
Tewel Abers 3D 61
Thackthwaite Cumb 4D 9
Thankerton S Lan 2E 21
Thethwaite Cumb 3C 8
Thirlestane Bord 1E 23
Thomas Close Cumb 3D 9
Thomastown Abers 1C 70
Thomshill Mor 4D 79
Thornby Cumb 2B 8
Thornhill Dum 2D 13
Thornhill Stir 4B 40
Thornington Nmbd 2B 24
Thornliebank E Ren 3D 31
Thornroan Abers 2D 71
Thornthwaite Cumb 4B 8
Thornton Ang 3C 50
Thornton Fife 4B 42
Thornton Nmbd 1C 24
Thorntonhall S Lan 4D 31
Thorntonloch E Lot 2D 35
Thrashbush N Lan 3F 31
Threapland Cumb 4A 8
Threlkeld Cumb 4C 8
Throsk Stir 4D 41
Throughgate Dum 3D 13
Thrumster High 3C 90
Thrunton Nmbd 4D 25
Thundergay N Ayr 1F 17
Thursby Cumb 2C 8
Thurso High 1A 90
Thurso East High 1A 90
Thurstonfield Cumb 2C 8
Tibbermore Per 1F 41
Tifty Abers 1C 70
Tigerton Ang 1E 51
Tighnabruaich Arg 2D 29
Tillathrowie Abers 2F 69
Tillery Abers 3E 71
Tillicoultry Clac 4E 41
Tillybirloch Abers 1B 60
Tillyfourie Abers 4B 70
Timsgearraidh W Isl 3B 96
Tindale Cumb 2F 9
Tingwall Orkn 5F 99
Tinwald Dum 3F 13
Tipperty Abers 3E 71
Tiree Airport Arg 3F 91
Tirinie Per 1D 49
Tiroran Arg 1B 36
Tirril Cumb 4E 9
Tirryside High 2A 84
Titlington Nmbd 4D 25
Toab Orkn 2D 98
Toab Shet 5B 100
Tobermory Arg 2C 44
Toberonochy Arg 3E 37
Tobha Beag W Isl 4G 93
(nr South Uist)
Tobha-Beag W Isl 5D 94
(nr North Uist)
Tobha Mor W Isl 4G 93
Tobhtarol W Isl 3C 96
Tobson W Isl 3C 96
Tocabhaig High 4F 63
Tocher Abers 2B 70
Todhills Cumb 1C 8
Tofts High 1C 90
Tokavaig High 4F 63
Tolastadh a Chaolais W Isl 3C 96
Tollie High 4C 76
Tollie Farm High 2B 74
Tolm W Isl 3F 97
Tolstadh bho Thuath W Isl 2G 97
Tomachlaggan Mor 3C 68
Tomaknock Per 1D 41
Tomatin High 3F 67
Tombuidhe Arg 3B 38
Tomdoun High 1E 55
Tomich High 3A 66
(nr Cannich)
Tomich High 2E 77
(nr Invergordon)
Tomich High 3B 84
(nr Lairg)
Tomintoul Mor 4C 68
Tomnavoulin Mor 3D 69
Tomsléibhe Arg 4D 45
Tongland Dum 2B 6
Tongue High 2A 88
Torbeg N Ayr 3F 17
Torbothie N Lan 4A 32
Tore High 4D 77
Torgyle High 4A 66
Torinturk Arg 3C 28
Torlum W Isl 2G 93
Torlundy High 4E 55
Tormitchell S Ayr 2D 11
Tormore High 1F 53
Tormore N Ayr 2F 17
Tornagrain High 1E 67
Tornaveen Abers 1B 60
Torness High 3C 66
Torpenhow Cumb 4B 8
Torphichen W Lot 2B 32
Torphins Abers 1B 60
Torra Arg 4D 27
Torran High 1E 63
Torrance E Dun 2E 31
Torrans Arg 1B 36
Torranyard N Ayr 1E 19
Torridon High 4C 74
Torrin High 3E 63
Torrisdale Arg 2E 17
Torrisdale High 1B 88
Torrish High 2E 85
Torroble High 3A 84
Torroy High 4A 84
Torry Aber 1E 61
Torryburn Fife 1C 32
Torthorwald Dum 4F 13
Torvaig High 1D 63
Torwood Falk 1A 32
Toscaig High 2A 64
Totaig High 4A 72
Totardor High 2C 62
Tote High 1D 63
Totegan High 1D 89
Totronald Arg 2G 91
Totscore High 3C 72
Toulvaddie High 1F 77
Toward Arg 3F 29
Towie Abers 4F 69
Towiemore Mor 1E 69
Town End Cumb 4F 9
Townend W Dun 2C 30
Towngate Cumb 3E 9
Townhead Cumb 4E 9
(nr Lazonby)
Townhead Cumb 4F 7
(nr Maryport)
Townhead Cumb 4F 9
(nr Ousby)
Townhead Dum 3B 6
Townhead of Greenlaw Dum 1C 6
Townhill Fife 1D 33
Town Yetholm Bord 3B 24
Trabboch E Ayr 3F 19
Tradespark High 4F 77
Tradespark Orkn 2C 98
Tranent E Lot 2A 34
Trantlebeg High 2D 89
Trantlemore High 2D 89
Traquair Bord 2C 22
Treaslane High 4C 72
Tressady High 3B 84
Tressait Per 1D 49
Tresta Shet 2H 101
(nr Fetlar)
Tresta Shet 1B 100
(nr Mainland)
Trinafour Per 1C 48
Trinity Ang 1F 51
Trinity Edin 2E 33
Trislaig High 4D 55
Trochry Per 3E 49
Trondavoe Shet 4F 101
Troon S Ayr 2E 19
Troqueer Dum 4E 13
Troutbeck Cumb 4C 8
Trumaisgearraidh W Isl 5C 94
Trumpan High 3B 72
Tughall Nmbd 3F 25
Tulchan Per 1E 41
Tullibardine Per 2E 41
Tullibody Clac 4D 41
Tullich High 1C 64
(nr Lochcarron)
Tullich High 2F 77
(nr Tain)
Tullich Arg 2B 38
Tullich Mor 1E 69
Tullich Muir High 2E 77
Tulliemet Per 2E 49
Tulloch High 4B 84
(nr Bonar Bridge)
Tulloch High 3A 56
(nr Fort William)
Tulloch High 4A 68
(nr Grantown-on-Spey)
Tulloch Abers 2D 71
Tulloch Per 1F 41
Tullochgorm Arg 4A 38
Tullybeagles Lodge Per 4F 49
Tullymurdoch Per 2B 50
Tullynessle Abers 4A 70
Tummel Bridge Per 2C 48
Tunga W Isl 3F 97
Turfholm S Lan 2D 21
Turnberry S Ayr 1D 11
Turnhouse Edin 2D 33
Turriff Abers 1C 70
Turtory Mor 1A 70
Tushielaw Bord 4C 22
Twatt Orkn 1A 98
Twatt Shet 1B 100
Twechar E Dun 2E 31
Tweedbank Bord 2E 23
Tweedmouth Nmbd 4F 35
Tweedsmuir Bord 3F 21
Twynholm Dum 2B 6
Tyndrum Stir 4E 47
Tynehead Midl 4F 33
Tyninghame E Lot 2C 34
Tynron Dum 2D 13
Tyrie Abers 3E 81

U

Uachdar W Isl 2H 93
Uags High 2A 64
Uddingston S Lan 3E 31
Uddington S Lan 2D 21
Udny Green Abers 3D 71
Udny Station Abers 3E 71
Udston S Lan 4E 31
Udstonhead S Lan 1C 20
Ugadale Arg 3E 17
Uidh W Isl 3B 92
Uig High 3C 72
(nr Balgown)
Uig High 4A 72
(nr Dunvegan)
Uig Arg 2G 91
Uigshader High 1D 63
Uisken Arg 2A 36
Ulbster High 3C 90
Uldale Cumb 4B 8
Ullapool High 4C 82
Ullinish High 2C 62
Ullock Cumb 4F 7
Ulsta Shet 3G 101
Ulva House Arg 4B 44
Unapool High 4D 87
Underhoull Shet 1H 101
Unthank Cumb 3C 8
(nr Carlisle)
Unthank Cumb 3F 9
(nr Gamblesby)
Unthank Cumb 4D 9
(nr Penrith)
Unthank End Cumb 4D 9
Uphall W Lot 2C 32
Uphall Station W Lot 2C 32
Uplawmoor E Ren 4C 30
Uppat High 3D 85
Upper Badcall High 3C 86
Upper Bighouse High 2D 89
Upper Boddam Abers 2B 70
Upper Bogside Mor 4D 79
Upper Boyndlie Abers 3E 81
Upper Cuttlehill Abers 1F 69
Upper Dallachy Mor 3E 79
Upper Derraid High 2B 68
Upper Diabaig High 3B 74
Upper Dochcarty High 3C 76
Upper Dounreay High 1E 89
Upper Gills High 5B 98
Upper Glenfintaig High 3F 55
Upper Hindhope Bord 4A 24
Upper Kirkton Abers 2C 70
Upper Kirkton N Ayr 4F 29
Upper Knockando Mor 1C 68
Upper Knockchoilum High 4B 66
Upper Largo Fife 3D 43
Upper Latheron High 4A 90
Upper Lenie High 3C 66
Upper Lochton Abers 2B 60
Upper Lybster High 4B 90
Upper Milovaig High 1A 62
Upper Neepaback Shet 3H 101
Upper Ollach High 2E 63
Upper Rusko Dum 1A 6
Upper Sandaig High 4A 64
Upper Sanday Orkn 2D 98
Upper Skelmorlie N Ayr 3F 29
Upper Sonachan Arg 1B 38
Upper Tillyrie Per 3A 42
Uppertown High 5B 98
Uppertown Orkn 3C 98
Upper Urquhart Fife 3A 42
Upsettlington Bord 1B 24
Upton Cumb 4C 8
Urafirth Shet 4F 101
Uragaig Arg 4A 36
Urchany High 1F 67
Ure Shet 4E 101
Urgha W Isl 3F 95
Urquhart Mor 3D 79
Urray High 4C 76
Usan Ang 2F 51
Uyeasound Shet 1H 101

V

Valsgarth Shet 1H 101
Valtos High 3E 73
Vatsetter Shet 3H 101
Vatten High 1B 62
Vaul Arg 3F 91
Veensgarth Shet 2C 100
Veness Orkn 5G 99
Vidlin Shet 5G 101
Viewpark N Lan 3F 31
Voe Shet 5G 101
(nr Hillside)
Voe Shet 3F 101
(nr Swinister)
Voxter Shet 4F 101
Voy Orkn 1A 98

W

Wadbister Shet 2C 100
Wag High 1F 85
Walby Cumb 1D 9
Walkerburn Bord 2C 22
Walkerton Fife 3B 42
Wallaceton Dum 3D 13
Wallacetown S Ayr 3E 19
(nr Ayr)
Wallacetown S Ayr 1D 11
(nr Dailly)
Wallacetown Shet 1B 100
Walls Shet 2A 100
Wallyford E Lot 2F 33
Walnut Grove Per 1A 42
Walston S Lan 1F 21
Walton Cumb 1E 9
Wampool Cumb 2B 8
Wandel S Lan 3E 21
Wanlockhead Dum 4D 21
Wardhouse Abers 2A 70
Warenford Nmbd 3E 25
Waren Mill Nmbd 2E 25
Warenton Nmbd 2E 25
Wark Nmbd 2B 24
Warkworth Nmbd 4F 25
Warmanbie Dum 1A 8
Warse High 5B 98
Warwick Bridge Cumb 2D 9
Warwick-on-Eden Cumb 2D 9
Wasbister Orkn 4E 99
Watchhill Cumb 3A 8
Waterbeck Dum 4B 14
Waterfoot E Ren 4D 31
Waterhead E Ayr 4A 20
Waterhead S Ayr 2E 11
Waterheads Bord 4E 33
Waterloo High 3F 63
Waterloo N Lan 4A 32
Waterloo Per 4F 49
Waterside E Ayr 1F 11
(nr Ayr)
Waterside E Ayr 1F 19
(nr Kilmarnock)
Waterside Cumb 3B 8
Waterside E Dun 2E 31
Waterstein High 1A 62
Watten High 2B 90
Wattston N Lan 2F 31
Waulkmill Abers 2B 60
Waverbridge Cumb 3B 8
Waverton Cumb 3B 8
Wedderlairs Abers 2D 71
Weem Per 3D 49
Weetwood Hall Nmbd 3D 25
Wellbank Ang 4D 51
Welldale Dum 1A 8
Wellwood Fife 1C 32
Welton Cumb 3C 8
Wemyss Bay Inv 2F 29
West Allerdean Nmbd 1C 24
West Arthurlie E Ren 4C 30
West Barns E Lot 2C 34
West Bennan N Ayr 3A 18
West Burnside Abers 4C 60
West Burrafirth Shet 1A 100
West Calder W Lot 3C 32
West Clyne High 3D 85
West Croftmore High 4A 68
West Cullerlie Abers 1C 60
West Culvennan Dum 1D 5

Published by Geographers' A-Z Map Company Limited
An imprint of HarperCollins Publishers
Westerhill Road
Bishopbriggs
Glasgow
G64 2QT

HarperCollinsPublishers
Macken House, 39/40 Mayor Street Upper, Dublin 1, D01 C9W8, Ireland

www.az.co.uk
a-z.maps@harpercollins.co.uk

4th edition 2024

ISBN 978-0-00-865284-5

10 9 8 7 6 5 4 3 2 1

Printed in India